like it is

*To Daddy and Mammy
and Gabe and Sammy*

Special thanks to Haydn Price

like it is

MY AUTOBIOGRAPHY

Chris Needs

First impression: 2007
Second impression: 2011

The publishers wish to acknowledge the support of
Cyngor Llyfrau Cymru

Editor: Haydn Price

Cover photograph: David Barnes

ISBN: 978 184771015 4

Published, printed and bound in Wales
by Y Lolfa Cyf., Talybont, Ceredigion SY24 5HE
website www.ylolfa.com
e-mail ylolfa@ylolfa.com
tel 01970 832 304
fax 832 782

CHAPTER 1

Like It Is

The boy from the Valleys

HIYA! RIGHT, GET THE kettle on; make yourself a nice cuppa and cwtch up on the couch. This is the story of me. Enjoy. Ready? Cool, let's get going. So where do I start? If this was my radio show I'd have introduced myself by now, so what am I waiting for? The name's Chris Needs. Not Chris, sometimes Christopher, but to most I'm Chris Needs. As if you didn't know already!

I'm the boy from the Valleys with the funny hair and flamboyant clothes, the boy who wore make-up as a child, was the pride and joy of my mother and a total embarrassment to my father. I was happy if I could cut my mother's hair and cook, but hated school and loathed sport of any kind. I loved Wales – but I didn't fit in, and was more at home in Spain than Swansea, Skewen or Sandfields.

Not so long ago I was in a club in Cardiff, it was my birthday and some of the people there were buying me drinks. As you know, I'm not a drinker and by this time it was quite late in the evening and white rum was almost flowing out of my ears.

The more I drank the louder I became. I was told to quieten down or I'd be thrown out. This old gent sitting next to me said, 'I hear Chris Needs the radio presenter is in tonight.' So I said back to him, 'I am Chris Needs,' and he replied, 'don't be so bloody stupid – Chris Needs is nice!'

Well, nice or not, this is me – like it is. Chris Needs, the misfit from Cwmafan, the village affectionately known as the land of the moving curtains (well, that's what people in Port Talbot would say), where money was kept in a biscuit tin under the floor boards, according to my Nana.

That's not meant with any disrespect, but with great honour and pride. It's where I was brought up, a place I love very much and will do until the day I die.

Home

Cwmafan lies three miles from Port Talbot and, to me, it's home. There's nowhere quite like it. Today it boasts several chapels, just enough pubs to keep the customers satisfied, one or two shops and, I'm glad to say, still a fair amount of Welsh is still spoken.

Back in the late 1960s and early 1970s when I was a mere boy there was a wonderful array of shops in Cwmafan. I remember them all – Jones the butcher, Hunter's the butcher, Howard the butcher (in his van). The Needs family liked its meat. There was Sammy James up in Tabor, Johnny Bennet in Pwll-y-Glaw, and he had a van, and Lloyds Bank which only opened on Wednesday mornings – I could never fathom that one out.

There was a petrol station, umpteen Co-ops, (my mother's favourite food store or should I say gossip centre), a hardware shop, a hairdresser's, a wool shop and a library. The Community Centre was where we had our birthday bashes and where bingo was held. I remember the caller, Charlie Carter, always had a bag of numbers on his lap, none of this electronic gadgetry like you get today. It was always eyes down for a full house. Two fat ladies 88 – that reminds me of her from up – oops no, better not say, I might get into trouble! Then there was a police station, a bakery, Mrs Morris the Sherbet shop and I think an insurance office as well.

There used to be a lovely lady called Sina Lane who had a sweet shop in her front room. We children loved going there! There was a park in Cwmafan with swings, a swimming pool and a cinema called Ebleys.

There was also a cinema in Port Talbot, the Odeon, and I remember going there every Saturday morning. On the way I would call into a butcher's shop which was just around the corner from the cinema, where I used to buy half a pound of spam to eat while watching the film. Quite a few lads did this. The first film I recall seeing was *The First Men On The Moon* and afterwards I had to build my own rocket, so armed with loads of boxes from Will Hills' shoe shop at the end of the road I started building it in my father's garage. It never did fly – and I never went to the moon! But my love of that film did win me a rather natty prize. I entered a competition about the film in the *Port Talbot Guardian* and the prize was a Remington electric razor. Just the thing for an eight-year-old!

There was the YWCA and YMCA, a clinic and our doctor, Dr Edwards, whose surgery was opposite our house. There were numerous petrol stations and garages. In fact, there was no need to go out of the village for anything.

Growing up in Cwmafan was great – but like everywhere these days, things change and people move on and buildings get demolished to make way for progress, or so they say. There are, however, one or two landmarks in Cwmafan that will always stick in my mind, places that are no longer there.

Firstly, the railway station, which was located behind the petrol station. It was a fairly busy station and trains would come down from the Valleys, stop at Cwmafan, and then go on to Port Talbot and beyond.

When I was a very little boy, probably not much more than a toddler, my mother, and what seemed like half the village, were all going on an outing, a mystery trip. I was going too. The big day out dawned and my mother dressed me up in my best clobber and we headed down to the station.

In those days it was all steam trains, no diesel and, boy, did they make a noise. We were standing on the platform, waiting for the train and when it arrived I screamed so much and so loudly that my mother had to abandon her trip and take me home. I didn't calm down for an hour apparently and my mother missed her day out thanks to me. It was a story I was repeatedly reminded of over the years. How embarrassing.

Those were the days though, almost half a century ago, in the early 1960s. Funnily enough, if for a moment I close my eyes I can see it all – the Co-op, the garages, the shops etc. It's almost like being there for real.

I remember Sundays so well; the sound of singing in the chapels was simply magic and the smell of cooked dinner sheer heaven! My mother would be in chapel with me and my father at home cooking the dinner. He always cooked everything and he was so proud of his cooking.

Every year we always had new Whitsun clothes and we'd all walk with all the chapels behind a brass band down to the school where we'd sing hymns. I felt so proud and I loved the brass band. I was very proud of my chapel, Capel Bethania, and went three times every Sunday.

Each Tuesday night there was the Band of Hope. It was just like a youth club and a get-together for young Christians. The highlight of the year, though, was the chapel outing – our annual pilgrimage to Barry Island. We'd sing on the bus on the way there, often changing the words to naughty ones, but nobody minded at all, it was all good fun. How I miss those days.

The village has changed a lot over the years but not The Waun. Here, time seems to have stood still and resisted change and that pleases me. I will always have a close affinity with

Cwmafan. There's too much water gone under the bridge to let it all go.

My Mother

My mother, Margaret Rose, was a great character and a comedienne, and to be honest I relied on her to get through life – and I think she relied on me too! Like me, I believe she was always insecure, and I know she hated being in her sixties and so desperately wanted to be young again. She thought she had wasted her life. Nothing really filled it in her younger days but, boy, did she live her later life – and all through me I'm glad to say.

She loved telling jokes and had a great selection for all occasions – one or two I simply couldn't repeat here. I don't want this book to be X-rated so early on!

My mother thought the world of everything I did, and I am sure she envied me, too. Mind, she was also my biggest critic.

She always said she was sorry that she married and had children. She wanted to be a jet-setter, to travel the world and live in different places every week. You wonder where I get it from?

My mother was a wanderer and had very itchy feet. She would have loved to have lived in a caravan, moving on when she got fed up of where she was. She had no close family apart from us children, and my father of course. Her love of travelling and her desire to be always on the move was something she longed for all her life – right through until the day she died.

I had no maternal grandparents, she lost her own mam, my nan Katie, when she was just eight years old and her dad, David, passed away when I was just a few months old and my mother just 20 herself.

I'm told that my grandfather was a bit of a lad and had children from other relationships but my mother never spoke about such matters. They didn't exist in her eyes. One day someone told me they were related to me in some way. I mentioned this to my mother but she dismissed it straight away. Who knows? To be honest, I don't really care.

Throughout my schooldays my mother would push me and support me with just about everything I did or wanted to do. I honestly believe she considered there to be nobody in her life, only me. We were amazing friends, more like brother and sister than mother and son. I miss her company so much and her advice, but most of all the honesty and the undying love.

My Father

My father, Harold (Aitch, as everyone knew him), was a different kettle of fish. He was a man's man through and through. In my younger days he would call me Mr Wonderful, his prince. Once he walked from Port Talbot to Neath to buy me a record as he didn't have enough money for the bus fare *and* buy the record, as his car was off the road.

As I grew older, he soon realised that I was not a chip off his block. I was definitely not the son he hoped for, and life between the two of us began to turn sour. He would call me Shirley and threaten to make me wear girls' clothes to school. It never happened, but it worried me, and I genuinely believe he really hated me.

What a disappointment I must have been to my father. He wanted me to be rough and ready, to play football, climb trees and chase girls like any normal boy of my age. The sad thing for him is that I didn't do any of those things. I was simply being myself. His bitterness towards me never changed, but it never put me off from being who I am or what I am.

It was when I grew older and proved myself as a talented professional musician travelling the world that he mellowed, and the relationship between the two of us became more like father and son.

When the grandchildren came along, not mine of course, but those of my two brothers, he mellowed even more. It was strange to see him with babes in his arms.

I was more than a little jealous because he treated those small children like I had always wanted to be treated when I was young. My mother also idolised them, but I was still her number one.

The Needs brothers

There's a seven-year gap between each of the three Needs brothers. I was the eldest and just seven when brother number one came along. He was seven when my youngest brother was born. I never really hit it off with my middle brother. We never saw eye to eye and at times it was quite difficult. I felt an air of disapproval.

My youngest brother, well that's a different story. I loved him so much and was willing to die for him and I really did my best for him, but later in life things went pear-shaped with him, too, and I grieve even now when I think of him, his family and what they are doing.

My father died in 1996 and of course everything was left to my mother. When she died in 2000 she left virtually everything to me. I was in such a state over her death that I didn't know what to do for the best. I respect her wishes for her estate to be passed on to me; she had her reason for doing that.

However, at the same time I desperately wanted to give something to my brothers, she was their mum too. My mind was in turmoil. I had to get over my mother's death before I could do anything, not an easy thing for me as we had been so inseparable. Sadly, the relationship between the Needs brothers grew ever more distant, and today it's quite a sad state of affairs.

None of us speak to each other. I would dearly like to put things right, and at some stage I genuinely intend to do so, but when people say to me, '*You shouldn't have to buy a brother,*' and other nasty things, I step back from it and try to avoid upsetting myself too much.

If the truth be known, I never needed the money or the house, and I would have preferred the entire estate to have gone to charity. They say that money is the root of all evil and, if I'm honest, this inheritance has brought me nothing but heartache. I wish it had never come my way. I would give my right arm to be able to put things right but I know this will take a miracle.

What hurts me most is not seeing their children, and that really upsets me. There you go, tomorrow is another day! Even though this rift has happened I still pray every night for all my family. Maybe one day things will fall into place. Let's see. Let's hope for the best!

I have a couple of cousins in Port Talbot but seldom see them. Lisa and Nicole – my dad's sister Hilary's daughters. They are quite proud of me I think, but our family has never been close. I look at other families and I feel a little envious. I want that bond, but I fear I'm never going to get it.

Just a radio presenter

I often wonder how my family and the village feel about my rise to fame. I don't think I'm famous, I'm just a radio presenter, but in the eyes of other people I suppose I am. I really don't like being well-known and I hate it when people who meet me act as if they are talking to a star or celebrity of some sort. I can't handle that. I'm Chris Needs, who happens to be fairly well-known, yes, but a star? No way!

I have found out at this point in my life that I really don't like being a celebrity, although I do love working on the radio. To me, broadcasting is everything. I wish I could be a bit like the singer from a band who people know of but never recognise. On air and when I am out and about I try to please as many people as I can, but in real life I'm quite quiet and, I suppose, a bit of a loner.

I like things to be right. I like etiquette and most of all I love my privacy. I love to see the people who pop in to my charity shops in Cwmafan, even if it's just for a natter. Sometimes they remark on how quiet I am, but there are times when I like to sit back and simply let others do the talking. Sometimes I'm just knackered, really, and resting.

I am a totally different person on the radio. At 10 o'clock each weeknight I come alive and go daft at the drop of a hat. I think it's because I can't see the listeners, but I can work out in a second what the person is like on the other end of the telephone. You paint your own picture of someone and I have a vision of all my callers.

CHAPTER 2

Early Memories

The Seven Winds

I HAVE GOOD AND bad memories of life as a child. Let's start with the good. My fondest recollections are of being at home with my mother. I hated school and wanted to leave so much that I regularly took an unofficial day off and just stayed at home.

My mother would usually always have lots of people back and fore to the house; friends or the odd cousin here and there, although there was never any close family around, other than Aunty Margaret Thomas to whom she was very close. She would always cook dinner by midday. It was always dinner, never lunch, for her pals from the Co-op, or for her cousin Afan, who used to work just down the road and would drop in from time to time for a meal.

Welsh was the language of the house by day, but in the evening when my father came in we switched to English as he didn't speak any Welsh.

I loved cleaning the house and cooking for my mother. One occasion still makes me smile; my mother's friend was celebrating her birthday and there was a party in Cwmafan Community Centre. So my mother, like lots of the other women, agreed to make some food for the do. My mother made a ton of meat paste sandwiches, not because they were nice, but because it was cheap. I was in charge of overseeing the sausages being cooked.

I must have been about ten at the time and as the bangers were sizzling and spitting in the frying pan I noticed lots of fat oozing out. Being the enterprising person that I am, I decided to pour the fat into a bowl, let it set then sell it as lard on little pieces of greaseproof paper. Sadly my idea never took off and I didn't make any money. Chris Needs the entrepreneur, eh? Well, at least it seemed a great idea at the time.

It reminds me of another money-making idea I had. There is a place known to us locals, us Cwmafanites, as the Seven Winds. It's on top of the mountain behind Brynbryddan. It's an odd name for a place, I must admit, but I'm told that it's called the Seven Winds because the air flows from lots of different directions at the same time – all a bit technical for me, but who knows, maybe they are right, I don't know.

Anyway, my mother and father would take me there when I was a little boy. It had just a single track road, and every so often along the way there were gates across the road. It was my job to open them to allow my mother and father through in the car and then close the gates behind them. My father always liked to play tricks on me and almost every time we did this he would pull off as if he was going to leave me stranded up the Seven Winds.

Often we'd go to the Seven Winds for picnics and also pick whinberries, or what we as kids would call wimbreeze, which I would sell for 2/6d (12.5p today) a pint, providing me with just enough cash to boost my pocket money so I could buy lots of extra sweets (otherwise known as fags!).

I don't think I could have coped with this puritan way of life without my fags so I smoked from an early age and loved it. I remember my mother saying to me, 'Damn, I haven't got any fags. I've run out,' in such a matter of fact way, knowing I would give her one of mine. Yet I was hardly more than ten at the time.

Like I said, my mother and I were more like brother and sister than mother and son – and we argued like brother and sister, too. Usually over something very petty, like clothes, handbags, make-up and hair products.

I used to do my mother's hair for her, which unlike mine was dead straight. She always told me that she had sex with the band leader Edmundo Ross and that was why I had Afro hair. For a while I believed her!

Not a great animal lover

One day the three of us, that's my mother, my father and I, went to Bristol Zoo, and my father, being my father, got bored very quickly. After looking at the animals he decided to take a rest, leaving my mother and me to wander around on our own.

I spotted an elephant called Rosie which visitors were allowed to ride. My father joked that the elephant was named after my mother as at that time she was, how shall I say this, carrying a fair bit of weight.

We ignored his warning that the poor elephant wouldn't stand the weight of both me and my mother, and off we went for a ride on Rosie, with my mother calling my father a few choice names. It was the first time I'd ever sat on an elephant and both my mother and I had a great time but my father kept insisting that we'd harm the elephant.

Can you imagine our shock and horror a few days later when we read an article in the paper saying that Rosie had died? My mother cried for days and I had to convince her that the elephant didn't die from carrying her. But then again....

Another animal I fondly recall was Jimmy, my tortoise from Ponty market. I loved Jimmy with all my heart and hated it when the time came each year for him to hibernate. He had a nest of his own in the ground between our house and next door, where he would spend the winter. I remember sitting and talking to him while he was sleeping, longing for the day when he would wake up again.

Well, imagine my surprise one day when I went out to speak to him and found that our neighbour had built a garage over the exact spot where Jimmy was hibernating. They have knocked the garage down now, and I half expect to see him coming out 20 foot around! That would be great as I never saw my poor Jimmy again. I was truly devastated and cannot possibly say here what I called the man next door (but to give you a clue I called him this even though his parents *were* married!)

I also had a goldfish called Bessie who I used to spin around in its goldfish bowl by putting my hand in the water and whirling it around really fast. My mother would say, 'Touch that goldfish again and I'll bloody drown it!'

So I'm not a great animal lover. I prefer them on a plate with some potatoes, veg and gravy. Just lately I'm starting to mellow a little thanks to Sammy, my godson, who has a dog called Harry. I'll tell you more about Sammy later, but the youngster thinks Harry is his brother.

On one occasion I had been looking after Harry when Sammy and his parents went away. I came in from work in the early hours, as is usual for me, and looked for the dog to give him a late-night snack. He normally had something like sirloin steak and chips. (Well, fair play poor dab, it was his holiday as well!)

But there was no sign of him and pretty soon I was starting to get worried in case something had happened to him. It turned out that he'd gone back home to Sammy, but it was a bit of an eye-opener because I really missed Harry being around the house.

My first studio

As a child my big escape was my bedroom. My father spent a lot of time building a fitted wardrobe and boy did I feel proper posh when it was finished. One day I put my record player inside and pretended it was a radio station, a silly thing to do I know – but look where it got me!

My room was like a self-contained bed-sit, complete with television, telephone and my make-believe radio studio, which boasted two record decks, a cassette player and a mixer with two microphones. I used to have guests to interview and wanted to be like my radio heroes, the late great Alun Williams and Ryan Davies

I had a red light outside my bedroom door to indicate the microphone was live and my so-called radio station was on air. I am sure my mother thought I was running a brothel. I made a programme schedule and often had to leave people as I was 'on air' in the bedroom in a short while.

This was a fascinating thing for my pals to see. One day a friend called round and looked in my bedroom. I remember his words to this day, 'Jesus, there's a wonder the floor hasn't given way!' Sadly, my friends were only ever interested in the things I had, not me! This bothered me sometimes, but I soon grew used to it. I knew I was different from them, and there was nothing I could do about it.

Much later I had the first video recorder in Cwmafan, It cost me £987 in 1978. I must have been off my head to spend that sort of money at the time, but it made sense as I was out so much by night and missed many of my favourite programmes.

I used the bedroom as an office, too, and often had rows for using the phone so much. I had an answering machine in there and when the phone rang the machine would kick in. My father could never understand why I could answer the phone from my bedroom and be in Taibach at the same time.

As a child I always played with phones and speakers. I still do, to be honest. I used to get loads of bell wire and connect up as many phones as I could around the house. This was before we had a real landline in the house. If someone called I would be upstairs and I would phone my mother downstairs. She would answer it, bearing in mind this was only an intercom sort of thing, so there was my mother posing downstairs with this phone in her hand saying things like, 'Oh, you need Christopher to play in the Chapel,'... or she might say, 'How much have I won? £2,000?' (this was in the 60s). She never stopped living the dream. Sometimes she would pretend that a celeb had phoned and that she was invited out to tea with maybe Dorothy Squires. We were as bad as each other.

The Tardis at the top of the stairs

I was a child who looked at the world through rose-tinted specs, with an imagination like nothing on earth. When I had a Christmas present I would play with the box more than the toy.

One year I asked for a selection of cardboard boxes and an industrial roll of sticky tape and, boy, was I on my own. On the top of the stairs was a cupboard with two doors. I put circles cut out of wallpaper inside to make it look like the Tardis. I even slept in it one night and my mother, if she was in a good mood, would pretend to be an android. She really did live on the same planet as me. The Tardis is still there to this day and I've got one of the wallpaper circles in my present house which I have kept as a reminder...

I remember on another occasion my father made me a homemade go-cart (better known to us kids as a gambo), using the wheels from an old pram, which we steered with a bit of rope. But I had to be different! I didn't want the same as the others. I wanted seats on mine so it became my very own bus.

I was fascinated with buses. Aunty Betty (another of my father's sisters) was a conductress with the old Port Talbot firm, Thomas Bros. I also had a conductor's set. It was red plastic and I had a money bag, the lot, just like my Aunty Bet.

I would meet her on the bus in Cwmafan and jump on with my conductor's set. I can't have been more than seven or eight years old at the time, but I would go up and down the aisle charging the people a second time and they all gave me a halfpenny each. Sometimes I was allowed to change the destination board on the bus: Sandfields Estate, Cwmafan Square, Pwll-y-Glaw, etc. I even made a destination board for my gambo bus with names like Great Western Terrace, Salem Road and the schools. I loved gadgets and still do today.

In all, I had three Aunty Bettys – the other two being Aunty Betty Davies/Jenkins from Tabor, Cwmafan, and Aunty Betty Belgium. Aunty Betty Davies/Jenkins was married to Uncle Harry who drove the bus and she was also a conductress. I stayed with her when my mother was having my next brother or when my mother was working. She always fed me well, and showed me the trick about the tomato ketchup. When the sauce was nearly all gone and was difficult to get out she always put a bit of vinegar in the bottle and shook it like hell. It worked a treat. I really liked her.

Aunty Betty Belgium – wait for this – was the wife of my father's brother, Uncle Eddie. She was another nice aunty to me. Her real name was Berta but we called her Aunty Betty Belgium. (Eddie and Betty met after the war while he was stationed out there.)

When they came over to Wales they always brought fantastic toys, like a motorised dumper trucks with control on a lead. When my Nana Needs died I remember Aunty Betty Belgium saying, 'Nix money, nix money.' I don't really know what happened when the will was read out but, there were a few glum faces...

Terrific times

My Nana had a friend called Aunty Gwen who lived down the road from her. I can only remember her being an extremely thin woman who always wore a fur hat and a fur coat, with a fag in her gob come summer or winter.

She never wore her teeth and I remember Nana saying that

Aunty Gwen had no sense of taste. One day Nana was making sandwiches for all of us. There was just enough cooked ham to go around as a few extra family members turned up rather unexpectedly.

The next thing, in walks Aunty Gwen with her fur hat perched like a tea cosy and her massive fur coat, and it was sweltering weather. She said, 'Oh Liz, those sandwiches look nice. Do you mind if I have one?' Nana only put a lettuce leaf in between the bread and I said to my Nana that she'd forgotten the ham. Nana replied, 'She won't miss it. She can't taste and she's got the wrong glasses on to see.' Good days, I tell you.

I was ten years old when my mother and father moved from Copper Row down to the Waun, and at the time my father was working in the steelworks and my mother was at home looking after me.

Money was short in those days and my mother was a little nervous of staying in this new big house on her own with me, a little boy. My mother's friend Mair Stevens (Jinks) would come down to stay with her when my father was on the night shift. We would all jump in the big bed in the front room, Mair, my mother and me. They would be telling jokes and singing songs all night so after a while I'd go into my own little bed next door.

In those days my mother had bad psoriasis on her foot and she went down to the kitchen to put some cream on, leaving Mair fast asleep in the big bed. I was half asleep and realized that my mother had fallen asleep downstairs in the chair.

The next thing I heard was the front door opening and my father coming in from work early. He went straight upstairs and jumped into bed, not realizing who was in it. Mair jumped out of the bed and darted downstairs. She said to my mother, 'Get upstairs and go back to bed. That's your job not mine.'

Another time it was a hot day and my mother was doing her usual thing in the shop and a lovely lady called Ella who used to live in Ty Maen Crescent popped into the shop. She told my mother that it was too hot for her, and she'd like an iced bath. Now Ella was only a little woman, so my mother picked her up and threw her in the deep freeze next to the frozen peas.

We had terrific times years ago and nothing really mattered. We just got on with it and enjoyed everything. It's a pity it's not a bit more like that today.

A child's Christmas in Cwmafan

Just like all children, the great love of my life was Christmas. I always had my toys put out on the sofa, never wrapped but on display for me to see when I woke on Christmas Day. I was very young and really did believe that my mother had sent a note to Father Christmas asking for the presents I wanted.

One year I was toying over what to have for Christmas. My mother asked me over and over what I wanted, suggesting things like a post office set or a tape recorder. I was dilly-dallying, trying to decide what was best and finally agreed on the post office set.

Like most youngsters, there was never any trouble getting me to bed on Christmas Eve, although I could hardly sleep as I was so excited. I could hear my mother traipsing up and down the stairs. Unbeknown to me, she was carrying the pressies down.

Ths particular year she knew I was awake, and told me that Father Christmas was at the house and about to leave my presents. I shouted back, 'Can I change my mind before he goes and have a tape recorder instead?' She was not at all amused and a bit of choice language came out, which was unusual for my mother.

Every Christmas Aunty Betty the buses took me to the works' Christmas party at Thomas Bros. Of course, she paid for everything and I always had an incredible present. Sadly, she is no longer with us.

Nana was another great giver of presents. She always let me

have anything I wanted, not just for Christmas, but anytime. I would say to her, 'Nana, can I have an album to save my stamps in?' and she would buy me not one, but two and a load of stamps to go with them. She was as good as gold to me. Sadly, she died when I was 14, and that was the end of an era. She was the only grandparent I knew, as my mother's mam and dad had died when she was young. She was eight, I think, when her mother passed on and only 20 when she lost her dad.

Sometimes my father's brother, Uncle Eddie, and Aunty Betty Belgium would come over from Europe before Christmas and they would bring loads of toys for us. Aunty Betty Belgium was funny and very extravagant as well.

Christmas was never quite the same when I grew into my teens. My mother would remind me that I was grown up and the toys and gadgets I used to get and loved so much were to be no more. 'It's clothes for you from now on,' she told me.

So gradually the sparkle and magic of Christmas disappeared. I naturally knew there was no such thing as Father Christmas, but I once kept a mince pie for years that I'd put out for him and that I'd found the next morning with a chunk bitten out of it. I genuinely believed that it was Father Christmas who had eaten it.

My Mother always got very sad when she saw starving children on television and so at Christmas she always bought a present and would send it to someone more deserving wherever he or she might be. She loved children so much, which was rather odd as I often recall her words about not wanting any of her own. Mind, with a child like me, who could blame her?

Christmas today

Today Christmas is very different with the roles reversed. I'm now the god-daddy – thanks to my godson, Sammy, who makes me feel like a million dollars.

Just like I was some 40 odd years ago, he now gets spoilt

rotten. He gets loads of pressies from me. I can still see his face as he opened them last Christmas. It was like history repeating itself. I love that little boy with all of my heart and I would do anything for him. Little Sammy has made Christmas so special to me again.

I tell him that I'm his fairy godfather, and he replies by saying he loves me. I can't stop him saying that. He says it about a dozen times each time we meet, 'I love you Chris.' I couldn't imagine life without him.

These days I tend to work on the radio on Christmas Day – in one way or another I've worked every Christmas since I was 14 – and always I regard it as an honour. I also like to visit hospitals at Christmastime. I've heard patients saying on the phone, 'Chris Needs has been here to see me…' and that gives me such a great sense of satisfaction.

People say to me that I must miss my mother on Christmas Day. It's true, I do, but I so dearly miss her every day. I feel close to her on Christmas Day though I don't know why. It's probably because she's having a tea party with Jesus, and celebrating with him. She always taught me to be considerate to others, especially at Christmastime. She always used to remind me there were people all alone, something I am only too aware of when I do my Christmas Day radio show. She would also say Christmas can be a dangerous time, 'good boy,' with so many people on their own.

On Christmas Day I would play carols at the piano, all requested by my mother who happened to act like my sister and we would sing our hearts out in the parlour. God, I miss those days.

I still look forward to Christmas because of Gabe, the man in my life, and his family and of course my beautiful boy, Sam. Gabe's mam goes a bit over the top at Christmastime and I get so many pressies from her and the family, it really makes me feel part of the extended family I never had.

Sometimes I feel that I'm her son as she leaves me out of nothing. I thank her from the bottom of my heart for that; otherwise I would be a right lonely boy without the Camerons. The older I get the more precious time is and I want to spent my life with people I love.

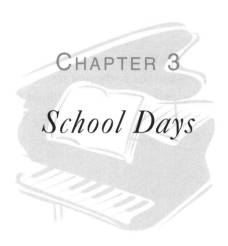

CHAPTER 3

School Days

Victim

TO SAY THAT SCHOOLDAYS are the best days of your life is a load of bull. For me school was without doubt the unhappiest period in my life. I hated it. I loathed everything about school, where I was bullied and called a nancy boy and prevented from learning.

Each weekend, when Sunday afternoon came around and the whole family sat and watched *Lost in Space* on television, I would get very tearful and quiet as I knew that the following day it was back to school.

I went to Cwmafan Infants and Juniors, both of which were lovely, but to this very day just the thought of Dyffryn Comprehensive in Port Talbot makes me feel sick to the stomach.

I was bullied more than anyone can imagine, not only by the pupils but also by some of the teachers, who were vicious to me. One in particular used to hit me across the head so hard with a piece of wood that it made me see double. I was a target simply because they didn't like me or understand my needs.

On many occasions I went home with one eye closed because it was the only way I could focus. I couldn't say anything about it to my father as all he would have said was, 'You must have bloody deserved it.' What a way for a youngster to live. I felt like a character in the film *Victim* starring Dirk Bogarde. I remember saying to my father when he was moaning at me one day for not being a footballer, 'Maybe you should look at the manufacturer,' and he went berserk. I thought I was going to go through the wall with the force he hit me.

My uniform was disgusting, I had to wear a green blazer and felt like a walking cucumber. I was very unhappy and was often picked on. All I ever wanted to do was study music and read. I never wanted to be like the others and certainly had no wish to chase girls, not that I didn't have the chance. I simply didn't have the inclination. I simply wanted to be me, but there were people in the school who were determined this wasn't going to be allowed to happen. I used to pray to God at night that the school would close or that I would be sent to a better school, but to no avail.

There were two boys in particular in my class in Dyffryn who really hated me and never left me alone. They made my life so miserable that I invented my own timetable to get as far away from them as often as I could. They would gang up on me, make fun of my 'girl's hair', hit me, spit at me, rip up my homework.

On the day I left school, I can remember walking down the long school driveway, past the head and teachers, all of whom meant less than nothing to me. I looked at them and said, 'You can't ruin anymore of my life, now. I'm out of here.' I spat on the floor and walked away.

Hope and ambition

Memories of those horrible distant days will always haunt me, but for every nasty memory there is a good one. My earlier school days were full of hope and ambition. I wanted to be noticed. I wanted to be different yet liked by all the other kids.

My first recollection is of Cwmafan Infants, and to this day I remember my favourite game in the yard, something we called Trains. We children would grab hold of the back of the jumpers of the boy or girl in front and we'd run around the play ground like a train, picking up passengers along the way. I loved it and it gave me my first sense of the thrill of travel, funny as it may seem.

Another memory was when I was about six or seven. It was St David's Day and we had our annual eisteddfod at the school. I was always in everything going, reciting, dancing, playing the piano. You name it, Chris Needs was in it.

I awoke early one morning on March 1st, really excited as I had about six things to do in the concert. It must have been about 4am and I was hungry. I asked my mother if I could have an early breakfast and she was half dead in bed. She told me to do something myself, 'Have you seen what bloody time it is?'

So I went downstairs and opened two tins of spaghetti, ate them cold and enjoyed it. I went back to bed for an hour or two, then got up, had a wash and made my way to school to perform.

My turn came and I stood in front of the whole school and started to recite a poem. Picture this: me in short grey trousers, sandals and a checked shirt, looking for all the world like someone from East Berlin, starting to recite 'Hiawatha Goes Hunting'.

'Then upon one knee uprising; Eye-a-watha haimed a harrow...' All of a sudden my stomach gurgled and I threw up over the side of the piano. All the children clapped. I had a thunderous round of applause. The children loved me and called for more.

One of the teachers, Mr Jones, looked at the mess I'd made and said, 'Go and see the woodwork teacher and ask him for some sawdust.' To thunderous applause I walked out of the hall, thinking to myself, now I know why there are woodwork lessons. Handy indeed. This still makes me roar with laughter today.

My favourite teachers were Miss Jenny Davies and Miss Verna Davies. They were great people who looked after us well. I felt safe with them and I could chat to them like talking to my mother.

Miss Jenny Davies invited me to her house to help me with my music. She nurtured me and encouraged me to learn the piano, which I loved. She was a very kind woman and so different from the teachers I would experience later on in my schooldays.

The headmistress was Miss Mini Lewis. She was lovely and always spoke in Welsh. She would call 'Chris-ter-foor' when she wanted me. I can still remember her Lyle stockings and the strict sense of authority she displayed but, that aside, I did feel safe under her wing.

Scales and arpeggios

Music was the love of my life, and when I was no more than five years of age my friend John started piano lessons, so naturally, I had to so as well. Miss May Williams (funny how they were all 'Miss' this or 'Miss' that) lived in our street in Cwmafan. She was getting on a bit and quite straight-laced and became my music teacher.

In my very first lesson, she showed me where to find middle C and I was away, totally hooked on the idea of becoming a pianist. I loved it and picked up playing very quickly. I have never understood why, but I could play tunes by ear, and read music just like I read English. I think this annoyed Miss Williams as I was learning too fast for her.

On one occasion she asked me what piece of music I would like to learn next. I wasn't sure, so she played a tune and asked me what I thought. I said to her, 'Let me have a think a minute,' while she went out to make herself a cuppa. By the time she had returned I could play the piece of music perfectly, just by having listened to it! This far from pleased her. I think she was upset about it and told my mother there was nothing she could do for me. I was totally un-trainable.

At the ripe old age of six I played the piano in the school assembly. The other children thought I was a star and to be honest I think was treated differently by the staff, simply because I was talented and could do things other children couldn't do. I loved it.

When I moved up to the junior school in Cwmafan things changed rapidly. I was expected to stand on my own two feet, and I wasn't sure if I liked this new, stricter environment I now faced. My first teachers were Miss John and Miss Lewis, both of whom were nice enough, but it is my last year of the juniors, in Miss Margaret Grandfield's class, that I remember now with most affection.

Miss Grandfield was very musical and trendy. She wore suede suits and high heels, just like a Paris model. Her hair was in a bun on the top of her head, wrapped in pearl-covered netting. It was in her that I found my soul mate – someone who helped push my piano playing to greater heights.

She wanted the best for me and, boy, did she push me. She's still behind me 100 miles per hour today. I remember my mother telling her once that she loved the gold necklace that she was wearing. Miss Grandfield promptly took it off and gave it to my mother. She was that type of woman, give, give, give. Happily she came back into my life when my mother died. At a time when I really needed someone like her the most, Miss Grandfield, now Mrs Bailey, would advise me exactly what to do and where to go. She told me I was still her little boy. I needed that. I am so grateful for her support and always will be. I love her so much. Today she is very much like she was all those years ago. She is a smart bit of goods, like an actress and I have so much respect for her.

Anyway, after she'd taken me as far as she could with the piano, Miss Grandfield persuaded my mother and my father to send me for advanced tuition with Mrs Aida Young Jenkins from Port Talbot, with whom I quickly became great friends – after a very strict audition. She didn't just take anyone, you know.

She was also an amazing person who knocked me into shape very quickly with endless scales, arpeggios and lots of difficult exercises. Mrs Jenkins encouraged me to create my own personality on the piano and I thought the world of her. It was because of her I passed all my piano exams.

One day, though, when I was in my teens, she caught me smoking outside and to say she was annoyed was a total understatement. She went spare. She said that my mother would not approve. I didn't have the heart to tell her that my mother often borrowed fags off me. Sometimes if I did my mother a favour she would even buy me a packet of cigs as a reward. But I passed every music exam I sat, and I could tell that Mrs Jenkins was extremely proud of me.

My first piano

Even while I was still in school the world of show business began to beckon and I started to get paid for playing in clubs. I finished with Mrs Jenkins and went off into the big, glamorous world of the South Wales club scene.

I was clubbing by night, and going to school by day. One day I was seen by what we called the 'whipper-in' (the boardy – ok, the truant officer, if you're posh!). I was in a café in school hours. I covered my tie with my pullover, held the fag I was smoking with my thumb and forefinger and blew rings of smoke into the air, which gave him the impression I wasn't a schoolboy.

That night I played in the club as usual and was told that the usual drummer was off sick and a replacement was on his way. To my surprise it turned out to be the 'whipper-in' and from there on we became good mates. It was an immediate end to problems of me mitching off school whenever I wanted to. He needed a few extra nights work drumming and I got him the gigs.

My first piano cost my father a fiver and he and my Uncle Arthur went over to Swansea to pick it up in an old, stinking van that was falling apart. On the way back Uncle Arthur had to brake sharply and the piano fell out of the back of the van, with half the keys falling onto the road.

Eventually they managed to get it back to Cwmafan and into the parlour. (No, not the front room, we never had one of those. It was always the parlour!) My father tuned the piano with an adjustable spanner, and I loved it. Everything I played sounded a bit like how Les Dawson used to play – you know, all the wrong notes – but it was still a piano and suited me down to the ground in those days.

My next piano was a Bentley Cottage Piano. It was a cracker and I had it until my mother decided to get rid of it when I went abroad to live many years later.

I now have a Roland electric upright piano, an electric baby grand like Elton John's, two piano accordions and a portable electric piano for stage work. (I don't think I will finish paying for all these until I'm about 152 years old and I certainly can't afford to die until then!)

Despite having bought me the piano, my father still wanted me to play football. As you can imagine, that didn't work out well at all, and to be honest the relationship with my father was quite an unpleasant one. Life was hard. I was striving to be something great and being held back by his macho views. What I didn't understand was that in the house he was so nasty about it all, but if I passed a music exam all he wanted to do was tell the world about it.

It didn't take long for others to hear about my musical expertise and soon I was known throughout South Wales for my piano playing. I once played for my Aunty Hilary's musical, which was such great fun. I even got a job playing at the Afan Lido in Aberafan, at a women's tap dance class and keep fit club.

I loved being in the company of women – mind you, some of them weren't really fussed on having 'a mere male' to play the piano for them. The chats we had included things like using thin bread for sandwiches and the price of clothes and hairdos.

The class was run by Marlene Evans (Boyle) and, boy, did she bring a taste of Hollywood to Port Talbot. I remember her jewelled specs and expensive hairdos. She became a great friend and often picked me up in her Mercedes sports car. I was proud of myself as all this time I was still in school but earning a few bob pocket money as well. I was the only boy in school to have a gold ring, a moped and a small fan club.

Anyway – I digress, where was I? Oh yes, school. Arghhh!

Dr Christopher Needs MBE, MA

I was devastated moving on to Dyffryn Comprehensive. The first two years were nothing more than okay, but then it went all pear-shaped. I was bullied because I liked music and not football, and some of the teachers would sit back and simply let it all happen.

Today, as I drive past the school on my way to the shop in Cwmafan, I always stick up my middle finger and say, 'Swivel on that'. It was a school that told me I would get nowhere in life. (Excuse me one moment while I take a break to stick up the finger again.) I hated that school and still do with a passion.

I spoke to someone from the school recently. They assured me that standards had risen there and invited me back. Well, I'm glad if today's kids aren't suffering the way I did, but that doesn't alter what happened to me. Nothing that goes on there today can change the hell I went through all those years ago. I have spoken to many past pupils and they agree. They say, 'Yes,

Chris, we felt the same,' but feel more sorry for me as I was more vulnerable.

When people ask me what school I went to, I'm reluctant to say. I don't want to be associated with it. I swear one day I will walk back in there and hold my head up high, though I'm likely to throw up all over the floor.

At a recent function a lady once introduced herself as the daughter of a member of staff of that school. I let her know just how I felt and made it quite clear that I had no time for him, nor any other member of staff with the exception of those chosen few. Thinking back on things, I firmly believe that if today's standards had applied back then, at least one teacher would now be in prison.

Not long ago I was in the car with Gabe, when he pulled up right outside Dyffryn Comprehensive. He asked me why I wanted to go there, and I told him I wanted to see the place that I felt ruined my life. After all the years that had elapsed since I left school I still felt physically sick when I looked at the building that gave me so much misery and heartbreak. Memories are made of this.

Despite what happened to me, and my hatred of school, I still passed 14 'O' Levels and four at Advanced Level – no thanks to that school! I continued studying when I was travelling, achieved my MA and went on to my doctorate of music.

My full title sounds quite posh, I suppose – Dr Christopher Needs MBE MA – but I only use it in its entirety when I need to give a reference for a friend.

As well as continuing music through the Associated Board London, and that was a tough course to get through, I also studied languages like mad, with the result that my Dutch is really good, along with my Welsh and Spanish. I cannot stress enough to youngsters today to get some sort of education – especially in languages, which are the key to the world. Being a Welsh speaker has helped me considerably, and speaking Spanish has given me years of pleasure, earning good money while soaking up the sun, broadening my mind at the same time.

Looking back, it's amazing how many of my fellow pupils have gone nowhere. Many have never been abroad, nor done anything much with their lives, and I think that is sad. They only needed a kick up the rump and they would have been away. My mother and my teacher, Miss Grandfield, pushed me like there was no tomorrow and I know how lucky I am to have had this nurturing.

To the youth of today I would say this, 'Make your parents proud. One day they may no longer be with you, but you'll feel that your life is worth something.'

I desperately wanted to phone my mother when my MBE came to light, but I can sit back and think to myself, she knows, and she is very proud of me. All I ever did was try to be 'a good son'.

I want my godson Sam to have a trade, hopefully one in which he can wear a nice posh suit and have a big shiny car to drive around in. I would love to see him in the media, making a name for himself. If that were to come true I would die a happy chappy.

CHAPTER 4

Coping With Being Different

The first man in Cwmafan to wear an earring

WHEN I WAS YOUNGER I felt so inferior to others that I needed to be noticed, so I always went overboard with my clothes. I still do to this day. I always thought that clothes maketh the man, which of course is not true. And when I went out, wherever I went, I had to be the belle of the ball.

When people said, 'You know the one, the one with the wild clothes,' that was always me. I had Carnaby Street-styled jackets and always had a shoulder bag to keep my aftershaves in, and my fags of course, my make-up, mascara and tissues.

I wore platform shoes, which gave me seven inches extra height, and flared trousers that almost took off in the wind. As my hair is naturally curly, I looked like Jimi Hendrix. There is no way people thought I was from Cwmafan. Probably up England way, I suppose.

To be honest I was the talk of the village, and quite often heard people say, 'There's something wrong with that boy,' or, 'Thank God he's not my son.' I tried my best to be normal, but it just wouldn't happen. I stood out like a sore thumb – but that was me, like it or not.

I love wearing foreign clothes and quite often in my younger days I would put on an Indian outfit to go clubbing in Swansea, always making sure I had my ciggy in a cigarette holder. I have lots of Moroccan clothes – jellabas and bits of headwear like a fez or a turban – and once I remember wearing a kilt to a nightclub back in the 1970s and the bouncer wouldn't let me in. Then I had a brainwave. I spoke with a Scottish accent and he let me through.

I was the first man in Cwmafan to wear an earring, although my father greatly disapproved of this. How could he go down the club having a son like me? On the other hand my mother thought it was great and seriously believed I was right and everyone else was wrong. She would often say, 'If you want to bring a girl home, you can if you want.' (Moving swiftly on...!)

I also loved gold and had a gold ring for every finger – it took a lot of money to look that cheap. There was no way that I looked a Valleys boy, but I coped with this fairly well. I liked being different.

Here comes Emma Peel

My mother sometimes used to say to me things like, 'I've seen a nice shirt in Swansea for you; pink with frills down the front.' While my father would be lying on the settee, grunting away and disapproving, saying things to her like, 'Mag, you're turning this bloody boy into a cowin' flewsy. What will the boys say down the club?'

Despite this, I continued to wear wild clothes and felt it was the right thing for me. I would spend hours pressing my clothes to go out, and loved making an entrance everywhere I went. Heads would turn and I loved it.

I painted my nails, and put glitter in my hair. Clubs in Swansea would often come to a halt when I walked in. They even put bets on to see what I would be wearing that night. Often my clothes would go missing off the washing line but they couldn't be worn, they stood out too much, and I usually managed to get them back.

I would sometimes wear a see-through shirt to show off my

tattoos. I was definitely a wild child and I believe to this day that it all came from my mother as she, too, had a wild streak. At the age of 64 she would wear leopard skin tops and knee-high boots. She loved life and her clobber – just like me.

I wore leather trousers around the house and my father would say things like, 'Here comes Emma Peel.' I also had a long, leather coat, down to the floor. I suppose I looked like something from *The Matrix*, but that was years before the film.

I also loved sunglasses and had loads of pairs. People would ask, 'Why are you wearing sunglasses indoors?' and I would always say, 'Your personality is blinding me.' Today, of course, it is quite fashionable to wear sunglasses at night, though probably resting on the head as opposed to covering the eyes!

I remember once in Bridgend I went into a shop and the man serving was wearing a pair of very square, frameless specs. I wanted some and he told me that they had come from an optician down the road. Not being a Bridgend boy, I made him write down the address and draw me a map so I could find the optician's. I found the shop, went in and ordered a similar pair.

Then when I was in Berlin once, I saw some fantastic frames in a shop window, so I went in, but I didn't have my prescription with me, so I couldn't buy them. What do you think I did? I flew out the following weekend with the prescription and bought the glasses. Sad thing is I can't find them now!

When it comes to shoes, you are talking to Imelda Needs. I must have had about 50 or 60 pairs of shoes at that time, and I used to buy a lot from '501' Jean, her that sleeps on top of me (by which I mean the woman who has the flat above the shop!). God, I must have spent thousands on clothes and Jean fed my hunger for the clobber as she had a catalogue.

Winkle pickers were my favourite shoes and I wear them to this day. I have approached strange men in the street (NO, not like that) and asked them where they bought their shoes.

I guess I'm trying to look like someone else as I'm not a fan of the way I look, never have been and probably never will be.

When I was resident musician in a big club in Port Talbot, Taibach Workingmen's club, a chap came in looking good in a pair of pointed boots with metal tips on the front. I wanted them so much I persuaded him to let me have them and that night he went home in daps.

Later, when I lived in Jersey, I used to go to jumble sales and boot sales. They were like Harrods. There are lots of millionaires living in Jersey; in fact they say there are more per square mile than anywhere other than California. I got myself some fabulous Gucci shirts, riding boots, suits and jackets. Even now when I pop over to Jersey to see my friends I always make sure that I find a boot sale to visit.

In the late 1970s and the early 80s when I spent a lot of time in Ibiza, I worked at the casino in Ibiza town and also sang with the band. I loved it. There was one thing above all, though, that made me feel exceptionally good, and that was the clothes that were worn there.

I went to a nightclub called KU where the men wore bowler hats and fishnet stockings. There was also a spaceman suit wandering around somewhere as well. I worked there with a girl called Lorri Guppy, she was great fun and loved life, showbiz and of course she loved clothes.

One day she took me to a boutique that sold wild, outrageous stuff, and I bought a couple of boiler suits, a leather one and a glazed cotton one. I wore these all the time out there, and when the time came for me to come back to Wales, I decided I was not going to let all this clobber go. This was me and that was that!

When I arrived back at Port Talbot railway station, feeling down as it was freezing and raining, I was still wearing my leather boiler suit. As I walked through the streets of Port Talbot, which now even sells man bags, everyone was staring at me and laughing. I was used to such a reaction and took no notice, after all a lot of people took the rise out of me and the way I dressed. I jumped into a taxi and the driver was none other than Maid Marion who helps out in the shop, or Joyce as she was called then, and we hit it off and poured our troubles out to each other, putting the world to rights.

One day my father went mad and tried to dress me in what he classed as normal clothes, saying I was an embarrassment to him and that the 'boys down the club' were talking about me. In fact he threw me out of the house. Things were quite grim at times. It was hard being persecuted for being a bit different.

By now I must have more clothes than M&S. Quite recently when a television crew from S4C came to film me in my house we counted 2,091 shirts and 300 pairs of shoes. We started to count the trousers but gave up as the filming schedule didn't allow enough time. M&S is wonderful. I just look for things I like and just buy them, knowing they always fit and are wonderful for...how shall I put it...the boy with a fuller figure.

These days I'm more into tee-shirts and ripped jeans. When my mother asked me what I wanted for my 44th birthday I simply said, 'Ripped jeans, please' and I got them. I recently bought a beret from the south of France, and I love it, especially when I perform the character, Pierre le Cweer.

Mock my devotion to clothes if you will, but it has had its advantages. One evening many years ago when I was driving from Cwmafan to a very important gig, the police stopped me for not wearing a seatbelt. I told the officer straight, 'I can't wear a seatbelt, it would ruin my new silk shirt.' He said, 'Oh, fair enough, Chris. Go knock 'em dead.'

I will die with straight hair

My hair is the bane of my life. It grows up and out and won't even get wet when I go swimming, the water just bounces off. The children in school would call me names, telling me that I had wool on my head, not hair. I hated it. I wanted to look like every other boy but I didn't and couldn't.

When I was six or seven I wanted to be like The Beatles, but I was more like The Four Tops because they had Afro hair. Back in the 1970s when I was recording a television programme with Teddi Munro at HTV in Pontcanna, Cardiff, my mother was driving towards the studio when she thought she saw me outside having a quick fag. She shouted, 'You look sexy in those tight trousers,' but of course it turned out to be an Afro Caribbean man, not me. 'Honest to God, Chris,' she told me afterwards, 'I thought it was you from the back, love.'

I once bought a Beatles-style wig. I loved it and would wear it when I went away to somewhere nobody knew me. I felt a million dollars, and people would often comment about my long straight hair. I would reply saying I hadn't had time to go to the hairdressers and it just grew wild like this.

I pretended I could not do anything with it and then the night would be over and I would get in my car and drive back to Wales. As I got near to Port Talbot I would take the wig off, and there I was again, Chris curly Needs. Awful.

This problem with my hair has always haunted me, and I'd swap my life right now for anyone who had straight hair. Once I called a hair transplant clinic in Bristol and asked for new head of hair, at any cost. I was devastated by their reply. They wanted to use hair from my own body, so what was the point?

When I was a teenager I went to London to have my hair straightened – a lot of Afro-Caribbeans used to go for the same reason – but the specialists couldn't guarantee it would work successfully. I went home on the train, devastated again. I started wearing bandanas and hats to hide my hair, and still do today.

On another occasion I went to Neath to have my hair straightened. It seemed great until I went out in the wonderful Welsh rain and it curled right back again. I recently had it straightened again in Cardiff but, again, it quickly went curly. I have even used French straightening cream, but it doesn't work on the Welsh, love, believe you me.

When people say to me my hair is so pretty, too pretty for a boy, it destroys me, and people really make me sick when they say that they wished they could have hair like mine, because they can. They can just go and have a perm, and then when they are fed up they can let it grow out again.

I've been told that if I have any more treatment on my hair I will lose it, but I've just booked again to have another go. Thinking about it, the less hair I have the more I will probably like it. I'm glad that cropped hair is more fashionable now and recently I've been thinking of shaving my head. Shall I? The clippers are quite handy....

Over the years I must have spent more than £100,000 straightening my hair – and it's still a curly Afro style. But I won't give up. NO WAY, MATE! One thing I can assure you – I will die with straight hair.

The man in my life

With my uncontrollable hair and my flamboyant clothing I am probably the most insecure person that ever walked God's earth. If I see someone looking at me from across the road I think they are after me or talking about me.

I'm paranoid about the post. I run to see if there's a tax bill or a letter about me that might hurt. I always feel as if I am going to lose my job. I am convinced that I am going to die soon and I try to make sure that all of my affairs are in order and there is nothing left around that I want to keep private. I'm also frightened that Gabe might trade me in for a younger model.

Oh yes, Gabe, the man in my life. He is the person behind the successful man. I could never have achieved any of this without him pushing me, encouraging me all the way. He gives me a reason to carry on and today there is nobody else quite like him in my life. He always takes a back seat, or waits in the wings, and is quite happy to do so as I don't think he would like my life.

I first met Gabe after he called for a dedication on Touch AM, the Cardiff radio station where I started my broadcasting career – well, unless you count my bedroom in Cwmafan. It was back in 1990 and I was living on my own in a rented house in Cathays. I remember how this chap phoned me. He sounded very nice and was quite an interesting person to talk to.

When he called I would play two or three records back to back so I could chat interrupted. One night he told me that he presented a programme on hospital radio, and asked if I'd I like to meet for a chat. I can't believe what I did next – I gave him my phone number and address, and he said he would come to see me the following Tuesday night.

I didn't know what to do, so I got my friend Sarah Holden, who worked on GMTV, to come around and said to her, 'When he knocks the door check him out. If he's nice ask him in. If he's not, tell him that I've gone out on a last-minute booking.'

The big night came and the door bell rang, Sarah went to answer it, she took one look at Gabe and said, 'Come in...'

Gabe came in and we introduced each other and Sarah had one drink and left. She had to go and clean the oven, she said. It was love at first sight. To this day I adore him, probably now more than ever. In fact I couldn't imagine life without him and his Disney collection. He is a Disney enthusiast, to say the least, and even has original drawings of sketches from the films and other various collectors' items (none of which are kept in the house – they are all in storage). But while he's quite an expert on all this, I just sit there and say, 'Oh God, more bloody cartoons again!'

I am a nightmare to live with – mood swings, unhappy most of the time, untidy, even rude, though I cook great food. We meet in the middle when it comes to music and travelling, but not with clothes. No way Jose!

Gabe is extremely conservative in his dress sense whereas I am like something out of *The Rocky Horror Show*. I bought some nail varnish once to paint my nails black like Robbie Williams. Gabe was disgusted, so I abandoned that idea. Anything for a peaceful, happy life. He likes to plan things so carefully, whereas I am quite happy to dash off to Spain for a drink at the drop of a hat.

Gabe's family have also been wonderful to me and have treated me like their own son. Gabe's father, Gordon, was a good mate of mine and supported me a lot in the early days. Once I had an accident and the front door slammed on my fingers, breaking three of them. I won't say what I said but Gabe's dad was there in a minute to take me to the hospital. He knew lots of the nurses there, and they were cracking jokes while I was screaming in agony. Fair play he was as good as gold to me.

Gabe was on overnights on Touch Radio when he called to tell me that his dad had died. I thought I was dreaming and went back to sleep, but Gabe phoned back and I jumped out of bed and took over on the radio for him to go to his family.

That was a night I'll never forget. My father wanted to help out with Gordon's garden as the two of them were keen gardeners, but this was not to be as my father died three months later. I miss them both very much.

It was a hard time for both of us, but we had each other and somehow we managed to cope. Gabe was wonderful to me when my own dad died. My father idolised Gabe and would take him down the club, and if anybody said anything out of place my father would create war.

My mother also thought the world of him and made him the executor and trustee of her will. When she died Gabe broke his heart just like I did, and I have to admit that if it wasn't for him, I too would be dead now. He has really kept my two feet firmly on the ground.

I also got to know Uncle Gabe – Gabe's Uncle who married a French woman, Jacqueline, and lived in France for about the best part of 50 years. He was a delightful man, in poor health, but we hit it off big time. The first time I met him I didn't know what to cook for him. He arrived here in Wales and I asked him what he wanted to eat. I didn't know how to cook snails, but he said, 'I could hammer a Clark's Pie'. Phew. From then on we became great friends. He would sit in my flat and I would play the piano and he loved it. I could see that he was not in the best of health and I did my best to look after him in the day while Gabe was in work.

We went a few times to the south of France to visit him and his family, and I loved the place very much – St Jean de Luz. Sadly, Uncle Gabe has since passed on, but I will never forget his words of wisdom to me. He always complimented me on my piano playing and that meant a lot. He's another one who is missed a lot, believe you me!

Gabe and I have been together for 19 years and I love him with all of my heart. He is my life, my friend, he's everything to me. I very much want to get married to him (it's called a civil partnership) because if I kick the bucket, I want Gabe to have everything I own. As the law stands, he's not strictly related to me, even though we have been together for nearly two decades.

Gabe comes with me when I am out and about in shows in South Wales and is a tower of strength to me. I couldn't manage on my own any longer. But I worry about him, because he's such a gentleman and is so nice to everyone. I don't know how he keeps it up. I'd crack and probably run amok if I were him. As I'm getting more known, so too is he. His life has changed dramatically since I joined the BBC, because it's 'Chris Needs this' and 'Chris Needs that' all of the time. *'Oh, and you're Gabe? Nice to meet you.'* People treat us like the dynamic duo, the Laurel and Hardy of Wales; we're like bread and butter.

Everything I do is for Gabe and if he needs anything I would be there for him. If he needed a kidney, he could have the two of mine. I thank God for giving me Gabe. It was one hell of a dedication all those years ago and little did we know that we would be together after all this time.

Gabe is the reason I get up every day and he is the one who keeps me sane. He looks after me with my shows and works on all the sound and backing tracks for me. He never gets jealous and just understands that I have to mix with lots of people, and at times, away from him. But there is nobody else in my life. Never have I been unfaithful to him and never will I be.

The trust that I have in Gabe is immense and if I came back in another time, I would still want to be with him. He's simply my whole life.

The boss upstairs

Gabe has great faith in the one above and so do I. This will never change. I was always brought up to go to chapel and pray. This was the doing of my mother – my father wasn't interested in the least, he just went to the club and to the bookies. I felt a great feeling of safety in Bethania Chapel, Cwmafan, and I knew there was someone else showing me the way. My friend upstairs.

Bethania has played a massive part in my life. We lived right opposite and you could hear the singing from the house. It was wonderful. I wasn't made to go on a Sunday, I wanted to go. I had great belief as a child as did my mother, though my father just kept quiet about things. A clever man, I hasten to add.

I am in no way a pusher of Christianity like some, and when people tell me they are a born again Christian I reply by saying I'm a first timer. I haven't seen God but I envisage him to be a man (sorry girls) with a beard and wearing robes, maybe an older version of Jesus. I have spoken with my Lord and have asked him for help and guidance and, I might add, I have had that help. My faith is strong and I couldn't go on without it.

Some years ago I was asked to read a Christmas blessing at a church in Cardiff for the gay community. I noticed this attracted people cast out from their own churches and chapels, and this made me feel very sad. I sat next to Lord Dafydd Elis-Thomas, a man whom I admire so very much.

When I am broadcasting I think my faith comes over and I hope this pleases people. I have never done a show without saying 'God bless you' at the end. I always say, 'Penblwydd Hapus Iesu Grist' on Christmas Day and on my birthday I always thank the Lord for another year.

For as long as I live I will trust in the Lord. He's not expensive, always right and always there. You're never put on hold with the Lord, and you never get asked to choose one of the following options. If time wasn't so precious these days I would still be going to chapel like I always did, three or four times a week.

The next biggest thing to God for me was the chapel organ. I loved playing it and the minister and deacons would let me practise there whenever I wanted. Some people were not that happy about me playing in chapel as I also played the organ in the clubs and they felt the two didn't mix. I suppose that was to be expected. You always get some objectors. I think it's called jealousy.

Before one particular service on a Sunday evening my mother told me to make sure I didn't show myself off and to make sure I played something respectful when the deacons went around with the collection trays. I thought it over, trying to come up with a suitable piece of music to play. I was having such a great time in the clubs that I decided that I wouldn't be a hypocrite and went along with her request. I played Tony Christie's 'Is This The Way To Amarillo?' It was the 1970s and I thought there were going to be heart attacks by the dozen. As for my mother, her face was classic. It's an image I will always remember!

There was another occasion when we were asked to wear our work clothes to chapel. This came from our new, young and mod minister, Ronald Williams. So, in true Maggie Post from *Pobol y Cwm* style, my mother wore her overall and I wore leather trousers, leather jacket and a purple frilly shirt. I wasn't out to make a mockery of the chapel, this was how I was and that was me!

My mother sometimes asked me to hold back in chapel, but I never did. I can still see her sat in the back singing her heart out. I used to pick her favourite hymns: 'Ombersley', *'Gwahoddiad'*, etc. She loved 'Arglwydd Mae Yn Nosi'. I didn't play this at her funeral and to this day I wish I had, it was just a slip up really. Thinking back, what I should have played was 'There's No Business Like Showbusiness'. That was my mother's anthem.

My mother always said that her boss was upstairs, and so is mine. I'm not frightened of dying. I know that I'll be back again in another body – this time hopefully a slim one and NO curly hair, hopefully in warmer climes.

My mother came back to me after she died. She sat on the edge of my bed in Cwmafan and said to me that if I carried on as I was that I would be dead by the time I was 52. I went to hug her and she stopped me, and told me that I couldn't. I thought for a moment that I was dreaming, but I wasn't.

The following morning I had a call from Gabe in Cardiff and he said that my mother had actually visited him in the night and told him to look after me. I couldn't believe it. It must have been right, she did appear. Then one of my mother's friends, Val Prosser/Cooper from Tabor in Cwmafan, called me and told she had seen my mother in her bathroom and had showed great concern for me. Well we all can't be wrong, can we?

Taking the tablets

I have always had a weight problem, which has affected me considerably throughout my life. I used to look at slim people

My mother and father, Harold and Margaret-Rose, on their wedding day, 1952.

Aunty Betty Downey (right) with her friend Megan.

Aunty Betty Downey, my father's sister (left), with friend Megan again, at Thomas Bros Buses, where they worked.

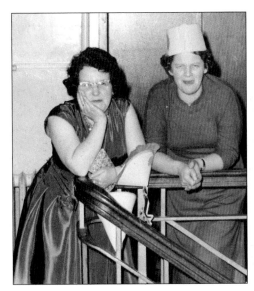

Megan (left) and Aunty Betty Davies Jenkins (another conductress).

My street in Cwmafan.

The Rolling Mill, Cwmafan.

Bethania Chapel, Cwmafan.

Co-op Outfitters, Cwmafan. I used to ask for boxes to play with from the Co-op.

Cwmafan Railway Station, where I screamed on hearing trains as a little boy.

Ebley's Cinema, Depot Road, Cwmafan, and next door, the YWCA where I went dancing.

*Taibach Workingmen's Club, where I was an organist for
many years – fond memories!*

*Workingmen's Club, Talbot St, Aberafan, where we had the Thomas
Bros Christmas party.*

Justine, Me and Maria.

'Countess' Christine and 'Lady' Kathryn.

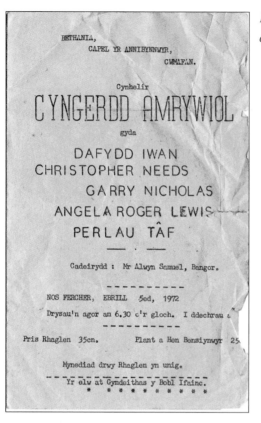

Memories are made of this.

The young impresario musician.

An early Chris Needs broadcasting.

Live at Big Buzz, Swansea.

With Goldie Lookin Chain.

The 'butch' look in Ibiza. The boiler suit had a few laughs down in Port Talbot!

Me in Ibiza, Spain – when my legs were good!

Duet in Spain with a local pianist.

Don't drink and drive – I might arrest you!

I left my horse outside the pub!

An early publicity shot – Chris Needs the pole dancer!

CHRIS NEEDS
INTERNATIONAL CABARET, TELEVISION AND RECORDING ARTISTE.

Hooray! I've made it to the BBC!

Young and innocent.

*Always smiling,
always posing.*

My wall of fame.

Cartoon by Jim – Crocodile Tondu!

Gabe Cameron

At the Hawaiian Club with friends in Jersey. I'm the third one from the left, if you don't recognise me. More meat on a jockey's whip!

Actresses Sue Roderick and Donna Edwards.

Christine from Durham.

and envy them greatly and begin to dislike myself a lot. I was a fat child and I was to blame in a way, I ate for Wales. But then there were no health foods available like there are today. My mother always cooked in lard or dripping, and my father had a chip shop. My mother also had a sweet shop and that did not help at all.

Once I decided to go on a strict diet. I had 15 weeks before we all went to Majorca for a holiday so I was determined to lose weight. I got hold of a book called *Dieting Revolution*. Each food item had different points and I was allowed to have up to 10 points worth of food per day. I stuck to the diet and when I felt like I was going to falter I would go out and find a slim man to admire and that would put me back on track.

I lost about three stone in 15 weeks. It made me feel so good. I remember buying a pair of trousers with a 26-inch waist. People would stop me in the street and give me the once over. I think that must have been the best time of my life. Sadly, as I got older the weight started to creep back on and today my weight goes up and down like a yoyo.

After my mother's sudden death I became irritable and ill. I suffered mood swings and generally I was not a nice person to be with. I put it down to grief, and boy was I grieving.

I started going to the loo to pee every 15 minutes or so and knew everything was not as it should be. After a lot of coaxing I went to the doctor and she took my blood sugar levels and told me she thought I was diabetic. I disagreed, and when the results came back I was knocked for six.

My sugar level was not high, it had gone through the roof. And weight was falling off me. I was put on tablets and I can honestly say that after half an hour of taking the tablets I was feeling more like my old self. I was so happy I called the surgery to tell them. The receptionist answered the phone and I told her I was no longer peeing every 15 minutes, I was back to normal.

It's very hard being a diabetic, as I'm often reminded. Watch your feet, watch your eyes, and if you don't behave yourself you'll have a leg off, or you'll go blind. It's hard when you go out for a meal and everybody else shovels the whole lot down and you are there saying to the waiter, 'Have you anything sugar free?' The answer is always no. Oh well! I have a plate of vegetables for my afters with olives. That certainly makes people stare, but there you go, nobody's perfect.

Quite recently I became very ill. In fact I thought I was going to die, so I went privately to see a specialist. I asked him if I could go on insulin, as I found it too difficult to do it all naturally on my own. He agreed I should be on it. Mind you, if I die I have made it quite clear that I want my ashes spread on Asda's roof. At least that way I'll get a visit from Gabe twice a week....

To this day diabetes concerns me. I speak to so many people on the radio and they tell me how someone has died of diabetes, or has gone blind, or has had a leg off. I really do try my best, and I know medication is so good today but, always a pessimist, I look on the black side.

Will I die like my mother did of a heart attack, one minute you're fine then, wham, you're gone? Or will I end up blind, or in a wheelchair? I will always remember my mother's words, 'Have everything, you might be dead in a week.'

I get lectured by Gabe and he won't eat cakes in front of me. It's not fair to him, but he really does care for me, so I stick to my special diet, lots of rice and pasta, veg and white meat. Boy oh boy, could I hammer a gateau.

CHAPTER 5

An Undiscovered World

Finding Catbrook

I OFTEN WISHED MY Tardis had been real. How I would love
to have been Doctor Who. Just shut the doors behind me, lock
everyone out, push a few knobs, twiddle a few switches and
I'd be off, far away from Cwmafan, heading for a different
life, a new undiscovered world. As a child I had a very vivid
imagination but I longed to be travelling for real. I loved going
away.

Every year my mother and my father took me to Tintern for
our holidays. It was the highlight of my year. We stayed in a
farm called Catbrook and the farmer's wife was Mrs Cleale. She
had a teenage daughter called Rosie and every morning Rosie
and I would collect eggs on this wonderful farm, which would
then be cooked for us to eat fresh for breakfast.

The drive from Cwmafan to Tintern seemed to take forever.
Trees lined the roadside and every year it appeared they had
grown that little bit bigger. Their branches stretched out far
and wide, almost like the trees were shaking hands with one
another. Occasionally the branches would block out the sun
altogether as they formed a magnificent green archway over
the country lanes.

Sometimes my mother's cousin, Aunty Mag, and Uncle Joe
would come on holiday with us and we would all play croquet
on the lawn of the farmhouse, with hens, ducks, dogs, cats and
all sorts of farmyard animals running around our feet. It was so

different, so very different from daily life in Cwmafan.

Not so long ago while feeling down and depressed after my mother's death, I suddenly had the urge to see Catbrook again, so Gabe took it upon himself to find where it was, so he could take me back to my childhood dreams.

The journey brought back so many memories, I closed my eyes and it was almost as if I was back 40 odd years ago, almost like I'd been coming here all my life. Sadly, finding Catbrook, (it sounds like a name of a film or something) was harder than anybody imagined. It was like looking for the proverbial needle in the haystack. We went up this lane and down another, and to be honest we were about to give up when I recognised some old gates, and lo and behold, there it was, Catbrook.

Sometimes it's not good to relive fond memories but here we were standing in the farmyard, the starting point for many childhood adventures. Everywhere looked exactly the same as when I last visited it more than 40 years ago, even down to the gates which were as I remembered them, as was the farmhouse building itself. It was as if I had never been away and I immediately burst into tears. Seeing the place once again made me feel good and a million memories came flooding back.

Talking of holidays, I am reminded of another family trip, a camping holiday in Oxwich, on the Gower, with my parents and their friends Thelma and Arthur Balston. They spoilt me something rotten, gave me everything. I liked that! I remember Arthur came back to the tent with a lobster, but his back was cut, he had slipped on the rocks trying to catch the thing. It's funny how little things like this stick in your mind! Quite recently I received an email from their son, Jason, who was only about six when we were on holiday together all those years ago. He told me he had a film of that holiday. I still haven't seen it, but one day....

As I grew older, holidays for me were usually working ones. I spent four years in Jersey on a summer season and I will always remember my parents coming out to stay with me for their own holiday. The first thing my mother wanted to know was she could play bingo on the island, and then she promptly spent most of her time with her eyes down and a marker pen at the ready. My father's first words were, 'There's marvellous, there's no tax on the horses out here.' Guess where he lived for the week?

One night I managed to get them out for a meal. All three of us went to this very posh restaurant called Winston's. All the time my mother whinged about why I had taken them to such a place, when we could have had egg and chips in a café at a fraction of the cost. The waiter came and, knowing that my father loved spicy things, I ordered him a peppered steak. When it arrived I felt so embarrassed when he asked for a drop of gravy to go with it. Well at least he said please, but these were times I shall never forget.

Way back as far as I can remember I had the urge to travel. I love Wales but my heart has been in a half a dozen other countries – all hot ones. To be perfectly honest, I am a roamer. I always will be. It's not that I don't like Wales, but I don't like staying in the same place for a long time, which is why I am forever popping over to Jersey, Spain or France. It's in my blood. My mother was the same; she could have lived in the back of a van.

Crossing the border

One lady who is very dear to me is Christine from County Durham. We met in Jersey and have remained friends ever since. Gabe thinks the world of her and once, when I was on a visit up in the north east, Christine took me to see a mystic, a lady who was into things like telling the future and reading palms.

We went into this old house which had no electricity, just oil lamps and candles. There was a funny smell too, like incense.

When the dear old lady appeared she welcomed me in Spanish. Strange, I thought as she was a Geordie.

She took my hand and asked what the hell I was doing here. I said I was visiting a friend, Christine. No, she said, here in Britain, you don't belong here, you are a mistake. She said I should have been born in Greece, Spain or Italy, and that I was homesick for these countries. She also told me that the next time I went abroad my life would be happier. She also said many things that nobody else would have known about, personal things about me, and things about my mother. She had to be real, she was so, so accurate.

I should be living in Greece, Spain or Italy, eh? That explains a lot. Ever since I was a little boy I'd been fascinated with foreign countries and their borders. No, not the sort you have in the garden, but those between the countries. I don't know why but that's how it is. You only have to mention a frontier to me and I'm off....

I remember seeing for the first time the border between Gibraltar and Spain. It was closed and I couldn't get across, but I desperately wanted to go across. I could see the British bobbies walking around and I wanted to be there too.

In those days, more than 25 years ago, you could only stay in Spain for a maximum of three months. If you wanted to stay longer you had to go into another country, get your passport stamped and then go back into Spain. Some people went to Portugal, others went to Andorra, and some went to Gibraltar. To do this you had to go from Spain to Morocco and then to Gibraltar. There was another way of getting there – you could hire a private boat, go out of Spanish waters and then sail back into Gibraltar – as if I'd do such a thing!

Occasionally I would go down to the border gates on a Sunday morning and listen to the banter between those on the Spanish side and those in Gibraltar. 'Hey Maria, your sister has had a baby,' was the sort of thing you'd hear. It was fascinating, but in those days it was often the only way to communicate between the two areas.

I remember the day the border opened. There were thousands of people there waiting to cross. It was so exciting. It is still very difficult to cross the border today as the queues are often horrendous and it can sometimes take hours to cross by car. Here's a tip: the best thing to do is park in Spain near the frontier and walk through. The first street you come to is aptly named Winston Churchill Avenue. Very British, my dear!

On one occasion when I walked through the border I showed my passport to the policeman and he just waved me through. When I got on the other side, I realised I had actually shown him my bank savings book, which goes to show how little notice they take.

For me, the most fascinating border of all time has to be the Berlin Wall. I went there in the 1970s and could not believe this huge wall that divided the city into two, dividing the east from the west. You could pay a few dollars to go across and the difference between the two sectors was immense.

The east was a very sad place indeed. I felt as though the East Germans looked at me with envy, as if I was a millionaire – which was probably right compared to their meagre existence. I went for a drink in a bar near Checkpoint Charlie where I noticed a young boy kept staring at my bottom. I couldn't understand why he was looking at my fat bum, but I soon discovered he was interested in my Levi jeans, the ones that used to have the metal badge sewn on the back pocket.

We started to chat but he seemed on edge, and worried about speaking to me, as there were people *watching from the Government*. His name was Fritz and he was considered to be a possible escapee. I tried to allay his fears and we continued to chat. I asked him what he found so interesting about my jeans and he told me that they could not get Levis in East Berlin. They were just not available, he said, adding that if someone did manage to get a pair on the black market they would cost a fortune.

I could not believe the things he told me and he asked if he could stay with me if he escaped. I said yes and gave him my telephone number and mother's address. He never did escape and I never received that call!

I felt so sorry for him and the awful situation he was in that I went to the toilet, took off my jeans and gave them to him. He cried. They were real tears, pouring down his face. That's what happens to me now when I think back about this sad but true story. At last he owned his own pair of Levi jeans, and the belt with a massive buckle which I gave him as well. He was so happy. He looked as if he had won the pools. I reminded him that if he escaped he could stay with me and I would look after him, help him with his English and try and get him a job in Wales.

I went back though Checkpoint Charlie wearing nothing more than my cycling shorts. Everyone seemed to stop and stare – but I didn't care. I felt a million dollars in that I had done the right thing and had made somebody happy.

Some years later I received a message from his cousin, who I believed lived in the western sector of Berlin. He told me Fritz would not be attempting to escape because of his mother. He couldn't leave her or live with the fact that he would never see her again if he did. He was too frightened to escape as he feared she would be punished. That is too all much for me. I don't blame him for staying. I think he is still in Berlin somewhere and one day I would desperately like to meet up with him and learn what he has been doing all these years, particularly now the wall is a thing of the past. Oh God – where are the paper hankies!

Last year a letter arrived at my mother's address from Fritz. He's now a record producer in Germany, he still has the jeans and at the time his mam was still alive. At some point I know we will meet up. I look forward to seeing those jeans even though I will never fit in them.

I flew to Berlin when I heard of the wall coming down in 1989, and the sights there were amazing. There were people reunited with their families after nearly 30 years. I joined in with the knocking down of the Wall and I have three pieces in my home today. I use them as door stops, but sometimes they get in the way as Gabe tends to stub his toe on one of them. I will never part with the stones as they mean a lot to me and bring back so many memories. People crying while being united – it was all too much for a Welshman, believe you me.

Paella, olives and snake soup

My love of travelling means that food plays a big part in my life, and the more foreign it is the better I like it – not that I don't love the occasional Clarks Pie and chips!

I am fascinated by countries and the food the locals eat. My ultimate favourite must be the Netherlands and the number one food from there for me has to be Boerenkool, a dish comprising potatoes and cabbage and a Dutch sausage wrapped in cabbage leaves.

I used to visit The Netherlands a lot to catch up with old friends I knew from Spain, Mieke and Wim, who live in Amersfoort. My, Mieke could cook! She loved her food. They are definitely people who live to eat, and that suits me fine.

I don't know how I know this, but Indonesia was once ruled by the Netherlands, which is why so much eastern-style food is eaten in Holland, things like bami and nasi, all superb rice dishes. I love them all!

If you listen to my show regularly you may just have heard me mention a place called Spain. Does that ring a bell anywhere? I've spent around 20 years there, on and off, and the number one food for me has to be paella. I cook it at home about three times a week and I remember trying to get my first paella pan home to Wales. It took a lot of planning believe you me. I had to have a foolproof plan for the pan.

Like most people, I only get Saturday and Sunday off work and I had to collect it one specific weekend. This was a problem in itself as the only flight I could get was from Gatwick and getting there alone takes three hours. Then it's a two-and-a-half hour flight and the supermarket where I needed to go closed at one o'clock lunch time – dinner time here in Wales.

It was almost impossible to do, so my friend Angie (otherwise known as Tressy – she has more hair styles than me) managed to get me a massive paella pan that would serve 50 people and leave it in my apartment in Gibraltar. Now, this is a BIG pan and Tressy is only a little lady, but after a lot of moaning and groaning she managed, against the odds, to get it there. I then faced the daunting challenge of making sure that I had a big enough suitcase to put it in. Somehow, I wedged it in on a slant, and eventually got it home in one piece.

I love olives and I was quite surprised when Roy Noble's wife, Elaine, told me that she too adores them. So when they visited me one day I showed her my cellar. It's crammed full of olives. I gave her some that I had brought back from the mountains in Spain. She was over the moon.

I remember once having a little get together in Cathays, my first home in Cardiff. My father had given me fresh beetroot from his allotment, so I boiled it and sliced it and cut up an onion with it. Sian Owen, Richard Burton's niece, sat next to it and ate the lot. There's class in them there hills you know.

I will always remember a very funny incident with my mother and my father concerning food. It was back in the early 1970s when the first Indian restaurant opened in Port Talbot. I used to go regularly to this curry house, but my parents kept asking me how I could eat such food. 'You'd be better off having a good Sunday dinner,' my mother would say. They both agreed that they couldn't or wouldn't eat any of it, but I used to come home after a show, and bring a takeaway with me knowing full well that my mother and father would love it. Despite all their concerns and objections they would both come downstairs in their night clothes and help me polish off everything. How people can mellow like the Madras they love so much!

Another time I was invited to a garden party at the house of Rebecca Evans, the soprano from Pontrhydyfen. I phoned her to ask if I should bring any food along with me. She said don't worry, there's plenty here, but it was up to me. So me being me, I took along two plate pasties that I had made in two new oven tins. When I got there I placed them on the table amid a lot of fancy food and a lot of influential people. Well, the whole crowd descended on the pasties and they went down a storm. To this day I haven't had my oven tins back, but I don't care, it was a great day and I think the world of Rebecca.

There was the time when Gabe and I went to Morocco – an experience I'll never forget. I loved it. We went around the Casbah and then on to this place for a fancy meal. The waiter brought out soup. Gabe loved it and had to ask just what was in it. They said snake! NO WAY, BABY! Gabe had another bowl and I ate the Pringles in my bag. *Ych y fi!*

Two great places to eat of equal brilliance are The Rolling Mill in Cwmafan, and Simon's in Gibraltar. Gabe and myself befriended Simon and Suzanne while restaurant hopping in Gibraltar. Once we went out there for two weeks and ate in Simon's for 13 nights. I loved the food there so much I thought I'd never find a place that could match it in Wales, but I did, The Rolling Mill in Cwmafan. Who says us Cwmafanites are not continental!

A firm favourite of mine is fish and I often grill some for tea – my main meal of the day, before I go to bed for my siesta. I have six microwaves in my kitchen, don't ask why, but I do – and I use them all!

Spain

My love affair with Spain started when I was 17 and playing with a band called Aquarius. I was their keyboard player and had to wear a penguin suit each night, which I quite enjoyed.

Aquarius were from Spain and on one occasion they asked me to go with them on a three week holiday. So off we all went and to be quite honest I didn't like it at all. I was quite a pain in the butt to the family with whom we stayed and longed to be home in Wales. Guess what? When I was back in the Land of my Fathers it wasn't long before I began to miss the Spanish weather and I had the urge to go back. Luckily I managed to get a job on the Costa del Sol as a pianist in a posh hotel. This was a major turning point in my life.

I was so fascinated with Spanish food, the people and the language. In fact, I used to pretend that I was Spanish and I studied the language in a class, which gave me the confidence to go out into the big wide world to try it out. I worked hard at the language and after three months I secured a job as an English teacher, teaching British children. It was not long before some Spanish children joined the school. I was then working in both languages. I loved it. At that time I landed a job as a translator, my Spanish improved by the minute, and these days I am probably more fluent in it than I am in English or Welsh.

I stayed in Spain until 1987, occasionally popping over to Jersey for the odd summer or autumn season, or back home to see my family, but I always yearned for Spain. Nobody there worried if I carried a handbag, or held my cigarette differently. The Spanish were more Chris Needs friendly than the Welsh. I could be what I wanted to be without being ridiculed.

One thing that is unusual is that the Welsh never mock me abroad. That only happens in Wales. Here I get called such things as nancy boy, poofter, shirt-lifter and other horrible things. This even happens now and I find it most hurtful. I don't think it's fair that my own people should mock me. It's my life and I feel I have the right to do what I want and live it as I want to, as long as it doesn't hurt anyone.

All my clothes, with the exception of a few, have come from abroad. My music is nearly all Spanish and most of my friends are in Spain and Gibraltar. Everyday I long to go home (I refer to Spain as my home). Life in Spain was good, until the call came that my father had died, and so I came back to Wales. Then the BBC happened, and the rest is history. I couldn't miss out on a chance with the BBC, so I jumped in at the deep end and put all my eggs in one basket.

I'm still here today, going for gold, but as I write this, I long to go back to Spain to live. I feel as if my heart is there. I know I will return one day. I've told Gabe that if I die before him I want to be cremated and my ashes scattered in Spain. So, whatever happens, I'll get there!

My chunk of The Rock

Gabe and I were on holiday in Gibraltar when the subject of postcards came up. I hadn't sent any. In fact I hadn't even bought any. So off I went to buy some. I was walking around when I spotted an estate agents. Ever the nosey one, I went for a look in the window and noticed an apartment for sale near the Rock, and overlooking Morocco. It was £60,000 and I immediately fell in love with it.

A moment later a man came over to me and asked if he could help. I gave the usual response that I was just looking. His reply was surprising. 'Are you from Wales?' he asked. You could have knocked me over with a feather. He told me that his son was in university in Cardiff studying accountancy. We talked for a while and then he said there was a problem with his accommodation in Wales and he was paying £900 per month for him and his friends from Gibraltar.

I mentioned that my friend Beryl had a house in Tremorfa

with three bedrooms and two lounges, one of which could be used as another bedroom and she was looking for rent of just £350 per month. He jumped at the idea and asked if I would call Beryl there and then. So I did. Beryl agreed and the deal was done.

The estate agent was over the moon and asked me which property I was looking at earlier. I showed him and he simply said he owed me a favour and suggested I look at the apartment next door, a repossession on the market for just £11,000. I couldn't believe my ears. I took out my credit card and bought it on the spot. We then went to the solicitors and I signed there and then. He told me that his other son would paint it for me for £50, and that everything would be settled in three weeks. I was on another planet. I only went out to buy some postcards.

When I returned to Gabe he was sitting on the bed reading a newspaper. He asked me if I had sorted out the postcards. Hell, I'd forgotten them. But I'd bought a flat instead. Poor old Gabe!

We enjoy going there and love being part of the community. When I go back the locals ask if I have been away. They think I live there. You must try Gibraltar, it's wonderful. It's like Tesco or Dorothy Perkins with palm trees and lizards.

Occasionally, I would be asked to stand in for someone who was off sick by acting as a holiday rep to pick up holiday makers arriving at Malaga Airport. I used to give a running commentary and then drop them off at their various hotels, Somehow I was always asked to meet the Cardiff flight. When the holidaymakers settled on the bus I would speak to the driver in Spanish on purpose, and then turn to the people, who by now thought I was a Spaniard, and say, *'Hello campers – no cowin' messing today alright?'* They would be in fits of laughter. The Welsh would follow me around everywhere and I was always showered with gifts and tips. They were very special days indeed...

Chris Needs and the Coconut Dancers

Closer to home, but far enough from Cwmafan, is Jersey, and the four or five years I spent there were memorable indeed. I remember driving to Weymouth in my Escort van crammed full of equipment such as an electric piano organ, my sound system and everything I needed to live over there.

The crossing was so bad even the sailors were sick. My mother had cooked me a chicken and just before boarding the boat I ate the lot in the van. Yum yum! Sadly I quickly realised this was not a good thing to do. Poor fish!

To me, Jersey looked very British and as I didn't need a passport I remember thinking it couldn't be all that exciting. How wrong this was to be.

I'd managed to get some work in The Hawaiian Club and I got lost trying to find the place. I stopped a farmer and asked how to get to Portelet Bay. He said it was a long way from where we were. It was at least three-and-a-half miles down the road, he said.

When I eventually arrived I was shown to my room in a house shared with dancers, singers, comedians, in fact all sorts of people similar to myself. Boy, was I homesick for Wales.

The owner of The Hawaiian Club, Chris Savva, was a Greek Cypriot and he wanted me to entertain guests in the Waikiki Bar and have nothing to do with the main show which was in the posh bit where you had to pay for entry. Night after night I did my usual thing and played the piano and sang in the Waikiki Bar. Soon visitors came from all over the island. The bar was always full and before long, people who booked for the show came to the bar for a drink. I was like a warm-up act before the main show.

By now many didn't want to go in to the show – they preferred instead to stay in the bar, and to hell with the rest! This riled the boss as he couldn't shift the audience into the main room. In the end he offered me a part in the production.

This was the first time I had ever done anything like this. I loved it.

One night the organist was ill and I deputised for him and sang as well as danced. The boss seemed to like this and although he was a man with a loud bark which frightened most people away, I got on well with him. We definitely had matching mouths. When he was in a mood he would shout at me, 'I'll keeel you, Welshman,' and I'd snap back, saying he wouldn't be the first man to try threatening that. He'd then burst into laughter. To this day we have remained good chums and I often stay with him in Jersey.

I returned to Jersey for a second season the following year. This time I was billed as Chris Needs and the Coconut Dancers. Again the Welsh came from far and wide, things were great.

It was at that time that I met Christine from Durham, who was working as a holiday rep. As I've already said we gelled instantly and to this day we are like two peas in a pod. Christine would tell the people when they arrived on the island that there was only one show to go to, that was The Hawaiian and, boy, did I pack the place.

The two of us were inseparable. Living together as well, though just as friends, of course. We often talked about what things would be like when we were older. One day I remember saying, quite out of the blue, we would have to stick together if ever we were on our own as we'd be company for each other. I love her with all of my heart and I believe that if she ever came back to Wales, she would want to live with me. Of course there is Gabe in my life, but he loves Christine very much too, and has said that he wouldn't mind her living with us. Life is too short to be apart.

There was a funny law in Jersey that nobody could dance on a Sunday. It was strange, really. You could go to a disco on a Sunday night and everyone would be standing around just tapping their feet, not dancing. Wild, I thought! The pubs were also open all day, unlike Wales at the time.

The Jersey people and I became hooked on each other, and some of them started a fan club. It was so funny. They even had tee-shirts printed with *Chris Needs* on them. I loved Jersey people and thought that I could live there had it not been for the strict property laws.

Jersey is a small place. I had mumps while on summer season in Jersey. As I was getting better, I wanted to go out but I couldn't as my boss would see me and wonder why I wasn't in work at the show. So my friend booked two seats on a plane to London, to see a show in the theatre…but…I had to get to the airport unnoticed and, as you know, I go nowhere unnoticed. So I wore a hood and dark glasses and wrapped a scarf around my mouth, and sneaked on to the plane. I did the same on the way back. The price of fame, eh?! It was a good night out, mind you.

It wasn't all plain sailing for me in Jersey. One day while I was there I discovered a lump on one of my testicles and immediately went to the local doctor. He sent me straight to hospital, where I had tests, and was operated on there and then. I was really lucky; the lump was massive and had grown in size daily. It was quite a thing to have cut out of me and I could hardly walk for weeks. I had stitches sticking out of my bits and it was getting me right down.

Of course, my mother was straight there and she spoke to the doctor, and had the lump put into a test-tube and kept it in the cupboard in Cwmafan. She looked at it daily, sticking two fingers up to it every time she opened the cupboard. She would say, *'How dare you try and ruin my boy's life?'* I suppose the message is never leave things to chance. Get to a doctor straight away. I'm so glad that I did.

Play 'Misty' for me

I have spent a massive part of my life playing in piano bars around the world. I've played in Lloyds in southern Spain and several in Puerto Banus. In Banus I always had the same American lady come to see me. She would ask for a Johnny Mathis song so I would play 'Misty' for her, and she would always give me a hundred dollar bill.

I also played in West Berlin in a club near where they filmed *Cabaret*, The Kit Kat Club. Very interesting that was. It was often frequented by people dressed in rubber but I stuck to my black trousers and frilly shirt, the standard cabaret look.

Many bars offered me work as I learned to sing a song in nearly every language. People would walk in, and I would always ask where they were from, and they would say places like Norway or Germany. I would immediately play and sing a song in their language. I learned these from the Eurovision Song Contest, so it does have its uses.

Teddi Munro and I did a stint one night while on a weekend away in Berlin. We went into this restaurant, Gabe, me, Teddi, and a couple who I met on a previous trip to Berlin, Andy and Ginge. We sat down and the whole place was still as if it was in East Berlin in the old days. People were still frightened to let themselves go, they still feared western ways.

There was a young girl playing the grand piano. She was about 18, very tiny and she opened her music leather case and pulled out a piece of music nobody had heard of before, real unknown classical music, and started to play. Well, I thought I was in someone's exam room. Everyone was so bored. As per usual, Andy, Ginge, Teddi and Gabe were saying, *'Get up there and show her what to do.'* But I didn't. I couldn't be that mean.

After a while she went and people politely gave a very dainty clap. So Teddi and I got up. She sang and I played some big band numbers. The place went berserk, clapping and shouting 'Ja, ja'. We'd done it again.

Today I always look for piano bars when on holiday; they bring back so many memories.

CHAPTER 6

The Saddest Days of my Life

There's only you

IT WAS A RITUAL. Every night I would phone my mother from a club where I was working to see if they were okay. I spoke to my mother the night before she died and I was so tired I wanted to end the phone call a bit quicker that I normally would have. What can I say....

I was having a siesta the next day at home, a bit of an afternoon snooze, when the telephone rang. It was my middle brother. We are not a very close family as you may have already gathered, so the moment he spoke I knew there must be something wrong.

He called to say our mam was in hospital. I could hardly believe what he was saying and didn't want to believe him either. I hoped he was joking, but he wasn't. He suggested I wait near the phone and he'd call when there was any further news.

Hearing what he had to say was a devastating blow, like a bolt out of the blue. I was stunned as my mother hadn't even been ill, and to hear she was in hospital was one hell of a shock to say the least. I didn't know what to do for the best, so I called my friend Maureen and she suggested I should go to the hospital to be by my mother's side.

I was living in Cardiff at the time and my mother was miles away in Neath. I phoned the hospital and the nurses suggested

I should get down there as fast as I could. 'Your mam is not a well woman,' they told me. I cannot describe how I felt, the shock hit me for six.

I jumped into the Jeep and drove off as fast as I could. I was low on petrol and not even sure if I'd get there. I tried to get hold of Gabe, but he was away in the north of England. As I headed west I was on my own, frantic, lonely, and needed someone at my side more than I have ever done at any time in my life.

I arrived at the hospital. My brother met me and told me to calm down. The nurse called us three brothers into a private room and said my mother was about to die. She asked if we would like to go in and be with my mother. I said yes without even thinking, but the other two, for some reason, did not go in.

I went into the ward where my mother lay in bed. She was barely conscious. I held her in my arms and asked her what the bloody hell she was up to. 'It's me. Chris,' I said. 'I'm here.'

She looked at me, smiled and said, 'There's only you. Nobody else. You are my life.' She then warned me about one member of our family in such graphic terms it really surprised me. Then, before she could add anything else, she slipped away in my arms. Her reason for such a strong comment was something she took to the grave but her dying words were something I would never repeat to anyone. She had no time for one certain family member, and to my mind, quite rightly so.

Confused, shocked, sad, and in great disbelief I stood there with my mother resting on my chest. I didn't know what to do. Should I lay her back down on the bed? To tell the truth I was frightened that I might hurt her. I was praying she was only sleeping....

The nurse then came in and laid my mother to rest, telling me it was all over, but adding she was glad that I had been there at the end. I know it's what my mother would have wanted more than anything – me at her side.

The hospital staff asked me to wait, saying the police would want to see me, so I waited protectively outside the room where my mother's body lay. The door didn't close properly and I was worried that someone might go in and touch her or something. She was defenceless and I had to protect her, like she had always done for me all my life.

I felt helpless and was in deep shock as I waited for the police to arrive. It seemed an eternity and my mind was in total turmoil. But, they never showed and I can only presume that they were busy with something more important. I felt let down and told the nurse I was going home to my mother's house as I was no longer able to stay there all alone with my dead mother in the room next door.

The hospital staff were insistent that I should remain there, but I had done all the bloody waiting I was going to do and said if it was that important then the police could catch up with me in Cwmafan. I went back to my mother's house and there was her cup still on the table, where she had left it just a short while earlier. I stared at it in a daze when the phone started to ring. I remember picking up the phone and with a feeble, quivering tone to my voice, I just said, 'Yes?'

'Mag, are you going to bingo tonight?' I fell to the ground, heartbroken. I told the caller the sad news and put the phone down.

I wanted Gabe. I had repeatedly tried his mobile without luck but thank goodness I managed to get hold of him. He was in the car so I suggested he should pull over so I could break the news.

He cried and cried. His journey home must have been really awful. I honestly believe her death cracked him up, almost as much as it did to me.

After what seemed like an eternity he eventually arrived in Cwmafan. Meanwhile I had called the BBC to explain what had happened to my mother. They were so supportive and told me not to worry about a thing, saying they were all by my side. Thank you so much!

Wind beneath my wings

Suddenly, after my mother's death, my brothers started coming back and fore to the house. Was my mother's death bringing us closer together? To be honest up until then we hadn't been close for a long time, but for a while we started to get close and I found that we were a great comfort to one another. It's a great shame none of us see each other anymore. Life's too short! But there you go; tomorrow is another tax-paying day.

My mother's funeral at Bethania Chapel was like something out of showbiz. I organised everything. Gillian Elisa sang 'Wind Beneath My Wings' in Welsh and when I walked up to the pulpit to say a few words I looked around and couldn't believe how full it was. There were top people from the BBC, pop groups from way back when, friends from abroad, Jersey, Spain, the north and south of England. I cannot believe how far people had come to pay their last respects. Even my mother's favourite minister, Ronald Williams, came down from North Wales to give a blessing.

I had prepared everything to say in Welsh and English. I made the people laugh when I said I remembered asking my mother should I go to the BBC. 'Yes, of course you should,' she replied. 'They could do with a bit of class.'

While I was walking out behind my mother's coffin, a woman caught hold of my arm and said, 'I'm sorry to hear about your mother...but has that competition question gone yet on the radio?' Talk about never being off stage.

I was upset after the funeral in that I never played all the tunes my mother loved. We had her favourite hymns, but I left out her absolute favourite song, Ethel Merman's 'There's No Business Like Show Business'. When I hear it now I think of my mother and tears come to my eyes.

I didn't realise it at the time – but there IS light at the end of the tunnel. It does get easier and it does get brighter every day – though the sadness never goes away. It took me three years before I could talk to anyone about my mother. I am sad to say, even dismayed now when I think back, that Gabe had one hell of a life with me. For days, weeks and even months I just sat and watched the same film, *Escape From East Berlin*, over and over and over, probably in excess of 1,000 times. Gabe was wonderful. He was a great comfort always by my side. I can honestly say I wouldn't be here today if he hadn't been so supportive throughout this awful ordeal.

To be honest, it was a bad time for both of us. My mother died on March 2nd, 2000, and was buried six days later. My birthday was just a few days later on March 12th and the following Sunday was Mothering Sunday. I remember walking into Gabe's flat carrying flowers for his mam. That was one of the hardest things I have ever done. I gave her the flowers and cried like a baby as there were no flowers for my mother. As I write this, I find it hard to control the tears.

Not long after my mother died, about two weeks I think, I plucked up courage to perform at a roadshow with Radio Wales in Neath. I stood on the stage feeling so lonely and full of grief, but hiding it well, and as I was just about to start to sing a fella in the audience from Cwmafan shouted up at me, 'How's your mother keeping, Chris?' Evidently he didn't know she had just died a couple of weeks before. I felt a stake go through my heart, but it happens.

Another time I sent my mother's car in for a service. It made me feel better to do that and the garage kept it in for a few weeks. When the car eventually came back, the garage parked it out the front of the house and the little boy next door said to his mother, 'Look Mam, Mag's back'. It is hard, sometimes, but it happens.

Dim damp o gwbl

After my mother's death it was soon back to basics with
the inheritance to sort out. The house was left to me, and I
never really wanted it. It has just brought me heartache and
problems. It is like a shrine and keeps opening wounds for me.
Every time I walk in the place I keep on looking for my mother
– and she's not there.

My mother was a wonderful person, and the biggest God-
fearing woman I have ever met. But she would tell jokes that
would make your hair stand on end. She used language people
might not approve of, but they are only words at the end of the
day.

A great Port Talbot word is 'cowin'' and is still used today.
My mother often said it after watching opera or ballet on the
telly – 'You can't beat a bit of cowin' culture,' she'd say. I still
howl at that. All the time she was seeking attention, she always
wanted to be liked by people. I'm the same.

Once, on a Welsh language television programme the
presenter showed her a photo of all the family and asked why
my hair was so different from my brothers. 'Different father,
love,' she said, without even flinching. That was typical of my
mother, just how she was.

It reminds me of the time when we were trying to sell the
house in Cwmafan. This was many, many years ago and my
mother asked a friend to watch my middle brother while she
nipped out to the clinic to get baby milk. The friend, Catherine,
said, 'This would be a nice house for my son', and went on to
ask if there was any damp. My mother said, 'No, not a bit...'

When my mother was out, Catherine decided to have a good
look around the house, to see how suitable it would be for her
son, after all there was no damp. *Dim damp o gwbl.*

Now, the drains in our street couldn't take heavy rain and it
just so happened that while we were out the heavens opened
up and the back filled up with rain water and all sorts of you-

know-what that came up through the drains. When we got back this poor woman was on her hands and knees with towels in her hand trying to stop the water pouring into the house. Her son never bought it. Dim damp indeed!

My mother once filled an application form for a job with meals on wheels. This was long before she had the shops, and she completed it as best as she could and how she though it should be done: *Eyes* – two; *hobbies* – bingo and cars; *sex* – now and again. I know it is often said as a joke but it's what my mother actually wrote. Believe it or not she got the job. I think people had more humour those days and looked beyond qualifications and whatever appeared on the application form.

Losing my father

Another sad time in my life was when my father died in 1994, quite a few years before my mother. I found out over the phone while I was live on air at Touch AM. I was playing a rather long record so I would be able to grab a few minutes to call the hospital to see how he was.

He had only gone in for a general MOT, to be checked over, so things should be really straight forward, I thought. When I got through to the ward the nurse asked if I was Christopher, the son on the radio. I replied yes.

The nurse then went on to say that my father had died. The shock was immense, I couldn't say a thing and I was on the air at the time. The nurse said she didn't think my mother had even heard the sad news so I called her and she was completely numb.

Somehow I managed to carry on until the programme had ended and left the studio straight away. God knows what I spoke about for the rest of the show, it was probably total gibberish, but then...

I legged it to my mother's house. She was devastated. We then went to the hospital to see my father. The hospital said not to touch him but I could not help myself. I needed to, I simply had to. I kissed him and he was stone cold. I had never felt such a feeling before, I wanted to shake him and wake him up.

I saw all the paperwork that confirmed all that had happened, but the really hard part was the nurse giving me my father's bag with his gardening books in it and his glasses and under-clothes. I fell to my knees crying like a baby as she took me in to a side room in a vain attempt to comfort me.

Not long after his death I began to feel ill and one night when I was doing a show in Barry I looked in the mirror to check myself over and my left eye was completely bloodshot. There was no white showing at all. I then noticed that my other eye had closed and my mouth was drooping on one side. I was so frightened I went straight home. Gabe took one look at me and said, 'Oh my God!' and demanded I went to hospital.

I had Bell's palsy and was put on steroids. I was very lucky. My face came back to normal within a week, but my mouth was a bit wonky and I talked a bit like I was drunk. Bell's palsy was viral and could be brought on by stress. I reckon if that's true, I should have Bell's palsy every bloody week, with the strain that I'm under.

It took a long time for me and my father to come to terms with each other. I was away donkeys' years before we ever started to get it together. We did, say for the last ten years of his life, so a lot of quality time was lost.

Thankfully, he really mellowed towards the end and admitted he loved Gabe very much indeed. That was nice to see. Now there is only me and Gabe, his family, Sammy, and of course my dear friends of many years and my precious Garden. Oh, I suppose I could always go down the club!

The anger

My mother and father went to their graves totally unaware of a major incident that changed my life for ever – me being repeatedly raped by a so-called family friend who was so dear to them. It all started when I was about five and lasted through to my early teens.

I have thought hard and long how to write about this horrific period in my life.

When I first put it down in writing I did so in graphic detail as I thought it was important to tell the story in full. But after reading it back each time it simply horrified me, and was unbelievable and far too graphic. Every word of it was true but it was all too horrible to put in writing, so I have decided to only give an outline of the events.

The man who raped me from the age of five or six made me do terrible things, and shall we say that not an area of my body was left alone by this bloody pig of a man. At times I bled, and was too frightened to say any of this to my family. I remember washing my pants out in the sink not to show my mother, just in case I had a row for it.

The worst part of being a rape victim is the anger. I still live with this every day of my life. I wake up sometimes in the night after a bad dream and sob my heart out. Today you can speak out to people. PLEASE DO SO! I COULDN'T.

Things are different now. If this happened nowadays he would most certainly be behind bars. But as it stands he's dead, and I thank the Lord that he is, so he can't do these things to anybody else.

His words still haunt me. 'Don't you dare tell your mother and father or you will be sent to borstal for being a queer.' I didn't even know what being a queer was.

The only thing that pains me now is that my folks never found out about this pig of a man. He got away with it, and here am I still suffering, and that will never leave me. I hope he rots in Hell, twice over.

Today you hear such horrific tales about child abuse and thank God there are many organisations out there to help. I hope nobody has to live through the things that happened to me.

The effect of this terrible act will never go away. I am still very frightened of aggressive men and gangs of lads. To this day I get frightened of some strong men, and I hide away from crowds, just in case I am set upon.

No-one knows what I went through. At the time all I wanted was to be alone and gather my thoughts and get over the physical and mental pain as best I could.

I honestly believe that the reason I am what I am today, a totally unhappy person, covering things up with comedy as best as I can, is because of him. He made me aware of this way of life. I knew everything about the male body and nothing about the female.

This man made me feel different about myself and this I will never forgive him for.

Rot in Hell. ROT in Hell!

CHAPTER 7

There's No Business like Show Business

Regular, Super or Supreme

MY MOTHER PUSHED ME into the world of show business. I really believe that she lived her life through me in that she was eager for me to do all those things she wanted to do herself but never had the opportunity to do. She desperately wanted to be onstage herself. Often she would want me to play the piano in the front room of our house and introduce her like a real compere might. *'Ladies and gentlemen; please welcome on stage... Miss Gypsy Margaret Rose!'* She would then sing something like 'Moonlight and Roses' by Dorothy Squires.

However, there was one song that took pride of place above all other songs and that was 'There's No Business Like Show Business'. When she heard that song on the radio, television, or in a film she would cry and say to me, 'I wish I'd never got married and tied down. I could be travelling the world now.'

She was probably the biggest influence of my life and possibly the wildest woman I have ever met. But compared with my mother, my father was quite ordinary; he was happy to go down the club for a pint and grow veg in his allotment.

I remember at one stage thinking about whether or not I should take up a day job in an office but my mother played hell with me for even suggesting it. In her sternest voice she'd say, *'Do you think I've wasted all this time and money on piano lessons for you to have a bloody office job?'* So the idea of an office job went out with the rubbish.

My mother loved her music and she had a collection of opera records, all 78s – you know, the brittle glass ones – which she often played, conducting the music on the Ferguson radiogram in the front room at the same time. My father had such a gutsful of opera being played all the time so one day he picked the records up and smashed the lot against the wall. There was uproar and eventually just for a bit of peace, he gave in and bought her a set of new ones. He towed the line after that.

Before she had the shop, my mother worked in the Regent petrol station at the end of our street. She used to wear a white coat and looked fab. I think she felt very much the business woman!

I used to go there from time to time and even today, after all these years, I still remember the price of petrol; Regular was 3/4d (17p); Super was 3/6d (17.5p) and Supreme 3/8d (18p) a gallon. No such thing in those days as litres, I'll remind you!

There was also no self-service like now. When someone wanted petrol, my mother had to go out in all weathers to serve the drivers, check the oil, put shots in the tank – and even work out the price in her own head. Men would flirt with her, especially the tanker drivers who stopped off for a cuppa and a natter. She loved it all but everything, I must stress, was totally innocent. To this day I think it was the attention she had that enticed her to be in the public limelight.

When she fell pregnant she gave up her job but a few years later she had the chance of having shop premises across the road from the garage. My father had retired due to ill health, a heart attack, and he'd had a bit of a pay out, which he gave to my mother, who decided to buy the shop, turning it into a most successful village store. Within almost no time at all the business took off in a big way and she bought herself a Jag, a new colour television – we were the first in the street – and had carpet fitted throughout. Posh, eh?

She had the most beautiful clothes, including suede coats, stunning tops and shoes, and like me today, loads of handbags. I still use some of her bags to this very day to keep different things in... They will never leave my side.

Ten ton of dynamite with a two inch fuse

Showbiz is a bit like the weather – always unpredictable. Although the money comes in handy everyone I speak to wants to tread the boards, that is work in the theatre instead of working in the clubs.

I guess I'm the lucky one. As you can imagine, working on radio, television and theatres I am constantly bombarded with offers of work and from people who want to appear on my show. I try to help as many as possible who hope this will be a stepping stone to their own individual success. I really do believe we have some wonderful talent here in Wales, but all too often I feel Wales gets forgotten, and this annoys me a lot. So I'd like to be the Simon Cowell of Wales, and support people as much as I can.

What upsets me more than most things is that many of the acts are of extremely high quality – yet, all my life I have worked in places that simply pay the money without even taking any notice what the act is. Please, don't get me wrong, some of the places were nice but others were very different.

I went to a rugby club in the Valleys once, it was about 30 years ago and the concert secretary was quite horrible to me, but he was not alone and that sort of attitude would leave a scar on me for a very long time.

Many years later I was asked to do the same club again but this time I was working on Touch AM, and was quite the

local celebrity. I did more or less the same camp humour as
I had done all those years earlier, but this time it went down
fantastically. Thankfully, nobody remembered me from the first
time!

Being gay was frowned upon in those days and hidden by
many people but I'm glad to say it's so different now and much
easier to be gay these days – even if there is still a long way to
go before people can live their lives how THEY want to.

I spent my youth hiding the fact I was gay and hiding
behind camp jokes. I regularly used to get hecklers but I had
some great put down lines. If someone male made a nasty
gesture towards me I would simply say, 'You're safe as houses.
It's only men I'm after,' or 'I saw you in the toilet, ten ton of
dynamite with a two inch fuse.' That would certainly get their
backs up.

During all this gay name bashing bit, one lady in particualr
helped me tremendously, and she is Marie St John the
songstress from Port Talbot. Marie sat up night after night
with me and tried to convince me that these cruel people in the
clubs that called me queer were not worth it and not to worry
about what they said. She is still today a great friend I'm glad
to say.

I never set out for an argument, I just wanted a chance
to show Wales what I was about, but most of the time the
'straight' people just laughed at me. This went on for years and
put me off Wales for a long time and was one of the reasons
why I set off for Europe.

I was accepted in other places for what I am, but this was
certainly not the case in my local club. You can't blame me for
having a few bad memories and gripes about some of the local
people who make up Welsh clubland.

Thankfully, I don't have to do clubs any more, but once in
a while I still choose to do the odd one or two. It keeps my
feet firmly on the ground, and reminds me what I am and

where I have come from. I sometimes do a show in the Dean Street Club in Newport. I love it there. It's where I can be myself and do what I want and the crowd love it, thankfully.

I am reluctant to park my car anywhere these days, so I am very selective about accepting certain club work. I don't know if it's jealousy or sheer nastiness, but my car has been attacked as often as five times in a month. It has become so bad that I always drive an old banger to certain areas – sadly that's all too often these days.

People often ask why I have so many cars. Its quite simple – the Jaguar is for me to travel to and from events; the motor home is for theatre trips, longer trips and jaunts abroad; the sports car (with the removable lid) is for the summer and gets used about a dozen times each year, if I'm lucky, thanks to the good Welsh weather.

Don't shoot me, I'm only the piano player

Show business is the only job where you can be at loggerheads with someone off stage and nice as pie to each other on stage and in public. My one big wish in life is for people to stop hurting me and believe in me and accept me for what I am. I always manage to get hurt, whatever I do and wherever I go.

Back in the days before I was well-known I would arrive at the club and start to get my equipment in and a committee member would say something like, 'I've never seen a nancy boy roadie before.' Who the bloody hell do these cavemen think they are?

Another typical comment might be, 'I hope you sing and play better than you talk.'

Once, a compere introduced me as, 'Miss, oops I mean Mister Chris Needs.' After that insult I then had to entertain the crowd. Boy, I missed Spain. The more I got knocked by Neanderthal committee members the more I wanted to go back to Spain, where I was totally accepted.

Just because I didn't want to wear a rugby shirt, or work in a factory I was singled out and persecuted. Once someone shouted out to me, 'There's probably been more meat up you than what's on you.' Mind you, I always had an answer for someone like him. 'Well you ought to know, it never touched the sides.'

The worst gossip can often be overheard in the toilet. Once when I was peeing in a cubicle I heard someone say, *'Well, what do you think of Larry effing Grayson tonight then, boys?'*

I was distraught by all this and longed to get out of Wales. When I walked out of the toilet the men would wolf whistle and say things like, *'Keep your arses against the walls, boys,'* or *'They sell Vaseline behind the bar, love.'* You might think that this is absurd, but we are going back to times when gayness was not accepted and this was the attitude of men who were full of booze – and couldn't handle it either.

Thank God I didn't turn out to be like any of those so-called men. I pity them, more so their poor wives for having to live with that sort of person in their life.

Most of my clubland memories are of drunken people – and I don't mean just the men. Very often the women were worse. I remember one woman bursting into my dressing room and trying it on with me. Of course, I didn't want to know, so I shunned her and simply said something cutting, like, *'If there were more women like you in the world, then more men would be gay.'*

I remember once being told to pee in the sink in the dressing room as some of the lads weren't partial to poofs around them! I was always the target for straight men who should have known better, who only wanted to destroy me – BUT NO MORE, BABY! Thank God they didn't succeed and I rose above it all.

Things started to get better as I became better known. After several years on the morning and breakfast show on Touch AM I noticed a big difference when I arrived at a club. For a change, concert secretaries would be complimentary and say nice things like, 'Bigger than normal turn out for a Sunday night'. It had been a long uphill struggle but now my name was going before me and that was a totally new experience.

People would tell me they loved the show and ask me about my Willy (the cat, of course). At first I was confused. How the hell did this woman in Newport, who I had never met, know about my cat? Then it would all fall into place – the radio.

The money started to get better and my confidence was beginning to show. From time to time I ventured back to those horrible clubs that had once mocked me and ridiculed me, but now they were completely different, and their attitude radically altered. Even those prats who once treated me with scorn came up to shake my hand. It was obvious they didn't remember me from my earlier appearances.

If you want to make a living at singing you must remember you aren't going to be in the London Palladium twice a week – you have to take what comes. There are lots of clubs around South Wales. I should know, I've worked in most of them. To be honest, I still enjoy going out working some of them today. It's nice to meet the people who are listening to me on the radio, and of course, there's always the chance of recruiting new Garden members.

Wonderful days

Don't get me wrong, there were some good times too. I have had many different and amusing experiences of clubs, far removed from the horrible, hurtful ones I endured for many years.

I remember going to a village hall in West Wales. I set my sound system up but couldn't find an electric socket to power up the system. The only one available was an old fashioned triangular type from what looked like wartime, so I ended up running an extension lead from the house next door and the village hall gave the lady a fiver for the lecky.

Swansea played a massive part in my life. It was where I took part in my first gig in the big wide open world. I felt safe in the Waun Club in Cwmafan, it's where my father drank, but this was Swansea, where everything was different, the people were trendy and talked differently.

I bought my first suit there in a shop called My Father's Moustache, it was a good local boutique. The suit was brown with stripes, flared legs and wide lapels. I wore a massive knot in my tie, just like Peter Wyngarde off TV's *Department S*.

I loved that era. I met the group Aquarius, the resident band at the Swansea Townsman Club and auditioned for keyboard player with them. They treated me like one of the brothers and it was like I had acquired a new family. I was left out of nothing, they taught me loads about showbiz, tips I still rely on today.

The group consisted of Aileen and her gorgeous husband Barry – everyone fancied him, he played percussion – and Aileen's two brothers, Reg and Phil. Although Barry and Phil have passed on, I still love them all. I feel as if they are related to me, and I will never stop loving them and all of their beautiful children. The sad thing is that they moved to Suffolk and it's difficult to get there with the scale of work I have.

The Townsman was run by the Wignals, and they were terrific to me. I felt as if I had a job there for life if I wanted it. I was really appreciated by the whole family. Sometimes Derek Wignal would take me to the casino across the road in High Street. This was amazing. I never paid for a meal or a drink.

I really miss those days. There were two managers working at the Townsman, Billy Reed, a tall blond handsome man, and Robert Sullivan, who married a singer called Gaynor, probably better known to you as Bonnie Tyler.

Apart from Swansea, I used to get work all over the area. It's strange really, but when my mother asked me where I'm working at the weekend – she always wanted to know where I was playing – if I said Magor or Chepstow she would say, 'How nice for you.' She loved Wales. However, if I said I was working in Bristol she would always say such things as, *'All that way to England, it's crazy,'* – and yet they were only a few miles apart.

Maesteg is very close to Cwmafan, in fact just the other side of the hill, but it might have been a different world for my mother. For starters, it was a different county, Mid Glamorgan, and we were West Glamorgan. There was a different phone book and people living there came under Cardiff with a CF postcode, where ours was SA for Swansea – and yet we were next door neighbours. Crazy!

Working in Maesteg was a touch of class. I worked at a nightclub there called The White Wheat. It was a snazzy place, with top acts on the bill, like Dorothy Squires.

Once they had the Brooke Bond TV chimps and I had to play for them. One of the monkeys sat quite close to the piano and was quite content until some idiot from the audience threw a banana which landed near the piano. You can guess what happened next. The monkey jumped on to the piano, ate the banana and blew me a kiss. He was a big brute of a chimp and I reckon he could have killed me. But the audience had a laugh at my expense, so that was okay....

I really enjoyed working at The White Wheat. The owner was a gentleman by the name of John Hockeridge. He was so supportive of everything I did. He knew that I had problems with certain male idiots in the club and he tried to help me deal with them. Even his dear lady Elaine tried to straighten my hair – now she was taking on an impossible task there!

I met a drummer at The White Wheat by the name of Ronnie Huxford. He was a fantastic musician and had played for thousands of artistes. Ron was probably in his fifties when

I first knew him and was married to a fabulous young lady by the name of Janice, who was quite a bit younger than him. For me, it was a match made in heaven. I knew instantly they were perfect for one another and they are still together after all these years. I spent a lot of time with Ronnie and he taught me so much about accompanying artistes.

While playing keyboards at Taibach Workingmen's Club in Port Talbot I met a couple called the Tambourine Duo. They were Randall and Lorraine, and were very easy to listen to and really lovely people. They sounded a bit like The Carpenters and we became instant friends. I was sick to the back teeth of meeting so-called megastars from all corners of Wales, but these two were just nice ordinary people.

We kept in touch and they often came to our house in Cwmafan to rehearse. My mother loved them to bits. We also met up at the Little Chef in Laleston, Bridgend, after a booking on a Saturday or Sunday. There were no mobile phones in those days so we had to plan this meeting very carefully. We would arrange it so that I was leaving Cardiff to head home to Port Talbot as they were, say, leaving Llanelli to head towards Cardiff.

We would rendezvous at the Little Chef and sit there for hours, scheming and planning and putting the world to right. We must have been all of 20 years old at the time. They were such wonderful days. I would be out very late, often not getting in until about four in the morning. One night I heard my father saying that he was sure I was knocking round with a wench somewhere. In your dreams, baby!

Another fond memory at Taibach Workingmen's club was a tenor named Bernard Plant, who sang onstage and halfway through his act he pulled out a massive snake. I hate snakes and during one songs Bernard put the creature around my neck. I passed out. The next thing I remember was a committee man giving me brandy and tea from a saucer. On the way out Bernard said to me, 'We'll have to do this again sometime.' No way!

Once in a while I accompanied a particular artiste who was a right pig. He had made rude gay remarks about me in the dressing room and lost no opportunity to take the mick. Having decided I was going to get my own back, while he was on stage I changed the key of one of his songs and he couldn't reach the top note. Nobody thought for a moment it was my fault as I was merely the keyboard player.

He stormed off the stage, shouting, *'That bloody organist is trying to ruin me.'* I went back stage and simply said, *'I wasn't trying to ruin you. I did ruin you,'* and suggested he went off to slag the next organist in another club. He learned a very hard but effective lesson.

CHAPTER 8

On The Radio

His Master's Voice

FROM A VERY EARLY age, I was hooked on music. I hated football, rugby and just about every sport you can think of. To me, life is for living and I wanted to live my life through music. Stuff sport and other boyish things I should be doing.

I remember our old radiogram. I would watch the record go round and round, looking at the words, His Masters Voice, and would be mesmerized by the dog. Even in those days I knew that music was everything to me and that nothing else would take its place.

When I was, say, about five or six, we lived next door to a man called Mr Rees, who I called Daddy Rees and his wife, Mammy Rees. They were lovely to me and Daddy Rees, knowing my love of the radiogram, made me a toy one out of a piece of wood and the lid from a Quality Street tin lid. The stylus was a table spoon and was attached with a screw. I played with this for hours and asked everyone for requests. I was a DJ long before anyone else.

My life was destined to be nothing but music. You will recall my father made me a fitted wardrobe in my bedroom which I converted into a radio studio, complete with microphone and red light. One Christmas I received a Dansette transistor radio from Dan Morgan's shop in Aberafan. I loved it and listened to Radio Luxembourg under the blankets at night. I remember how it used to fade in and out – and always during your favourite record.

Some years later I was infatuated by Swansea Sound which started broadcasting in the early 1970s. It was the first commercial radio station in Wales. Until then I had listened to national radio stations which always seemed to be about England. You would never hear any local names. Suddenly here was a radio station where disc jockeys talked about Gorseinon, Llanelli and Port Talbot, all places I knew.

Local radio meant everything to me and I knew I had to somehow get my foot in through the door. I became quite friendly with a presenter called Doreen Jenkins, who was originally on the afternoon show before moving to a later programme called *Nocturne*.

I always entered the usual competitions and from time to time even won the odd prize. One day Doreen invited me to the studios at Gorseinon. This was heaven. I went in and met her. I was shaking as she guided me around the building and she even let me sit in the studio while she was broadcasting. This kindled my great interest in radio. I wanted what she had, and nothing was going to stop me from getting it.

I remember being invited to Swansea Sound to do an interview about a big concert that was happening in Swansea. I was so excited and could hardly curtail my enthusiasm. I was going to be on the radio! I sat there in the studio, laughing and joking until the red light went on, which indicated we were on air. I froze. I made a complete *twp* of myself. I left the studio in tears, convinced they would never invite me back and that was the end of my short-lived radio career.

I think that I made a bit of a nuisance of myself by phoning them all the time, but even after making such a hash of things they were ever so good to me and put up with me. You have to get your foot in one way or other. This goes to show that if you want to do something for God's sake go and do it, otherwise someone else will sit in your seat. My mother always said to me there's always someone eager and younger ready to take over.

I used to think that whatever was said on the radio must be true and I simply wanted to be part of it – but fate stepped in and I moved to Jersey and then Spain.

Love at first Touch

In 1990 I came back from Spain and was living in Cardiff when a mate of mine, Steve Dutfield, told me about a new radio station, Touch AM (now Capital Gold). It was a sister station to Red Dragon and was targeted at an older age range with a more general mix of music. This was for me – my interest in radio had been re-kindled so I decided to make an audition tape on a ghetto blaster on the floor of my living room.

I interviewed a friend of mine, Li Harding, the fab female singer from The Root Doctors. She was so supportive and gave an excellent chat on tape, bearing in mind that I'd never done anything like this before.

I managed to edit the tape with next to nothing in the way of equipment and in all fairness I thought it sounded a bit of alright, so I posted it off to the programme controller at Touch. My fingers and everything else were crossed, I can tell you that!

I heard nothing for a few weeks and one day the call came, asking me to pop in for a chat. I was going to opt out because of nerves, but Li made me go for the audition, so down I trundled in my grooviest clobber and met the top man at Touch. He said he liked what I had done, adding that I was naturally very funny. He asked me if I would make another tape in the studios, so of course I jumped at the chance.

I didn't know what buttons to press or indeed what any of the equipment actually did, so I thought when in doubt get Steve Dutfield out. The poor dab did all the engineering work while I did all the chopsing. It worked really well and I was called back to have another interview. I was asked if I could drive (the technical term for operating the presenter's desk). Not knowing what he was talking about, I said, 'Yes, of course. I've got a Seat Marbella.' He thought I was being funny, but I hadn't meant to be, and he suggested I should start immediately with a weekly programme called *The Wenglish Show*.

I didn't do the first programme live, it was recorded and I remember listening to it at home. I immediately thought, 'Chris, you've made it'. It was the thing I'd been searching for all of my life. I was well chuffed. The following week I did the programme live and drove the desk myself. Boy, were my hands shaking big time, but my newly discovered love for radio pulled me through.

I was given the chance to do an overnight programme, between two and six in the morning, and I remember taking a sack full of vinyl records to the studio, as in those days I wasn't too sure how to work the compact disc player. One of the presenters, Jeff Thomas, showed me how to put a disc into the machine – I felt like a rocket scientist. There was no holding me back...

I enjoyed the overnight programme which continued for months on end. I remember a woman calling me up and saying she loved the show. I remember asking myself, what show? I hadn't sung nor done any comedy. I thanked her but her comments set me wondering. The radio was a powerful tool and it amplified everything I did.

In the clubs I would have to go flat out with a joke to get a reaction, but on the radio I could be gentle and laid back and have the same effect. This was something new to me, something I learned very early on in radio and it was a strange thing.

People would stop me in the street and ask if I was that fella on the radio, and this was quite unusual. Today I'm stopped everywhere, from Asda to East Berlin. I take it as part of the job and always try to please. My favourite line is when someone asks me if I am Chris Needs. I always answer by saying, 'Yes, *disappointing isn't it?'* I do like being stopped in the street; it makes me feel as if I have done my job well. If you ever see me out and about do stop me to say hello.

My time at Touch was a great learning curve for me. I lived in a street called Fitzhamon Embankment, which was across the river from Cardiff Arms Park (now the Millennium Stadium). I used to walk to work as it was only over the road about half a mile, but I had to stop walking as I was attacked once walking back home. Gabe used to cycle to the studio to do his night show, just to keep fit. I was worried that he might get done over like me, he'd never get away from an attacker – if he cycled any slower, he'd fall off. Fortunately he never did have any problems, but I had to move. I was too frightened to live in the city centre. Pity, I liked it there.

There were some fun times at Touch. When it started, in 1990, I had one of the DJs staying with me for a while, Mike Longley. One night Mike, another DJ Jeff Starr and I went down to a pub in Cathays. I had a night off and the following day and they were all congratulating me on my new show on air as this was my first radio job.

I sat in the corner and got slowly sozzled. When it came to go home, I could hardly walk. I staggered up the street, singing a Dot Squires song at full pelt. I lost my shoe, and fell off the pavement umpteen times – well, we've all been young! I got back to the house and we were all starving. I had run out of bread, so I decided to bake some, without the aid of a safety net, or a bread maker!

I managed to get the oven door open and threw in this piece of floury substance, waited on the kitchen floor until it was cooked and took it out. It was almost burned and I dropped it as it was so hot and cracked the oil cloth. That was my time to say, 'Never again will I drink.' While all of this was going on I think the other two nipped out for a takeaway.

A tiddler at the Beeb

My radio career at Touch continued to flourish, so much so that I was honoured to win the Sony Radio Award as Best UK Regional Presenter. To me that was like winning an Oscar. I was overjoyed and wanted everyone to know.

My first thought was to call Nick Evans, the editor of BBC Radio Wales at that time, but not surprisingly I could not get past his secretary, who told me he was busy. I could not believe it. Determined not to be given the cold shoulder, I was definitely not going to give up, I said in a very laid back way, *'He'll kick himself if he doesn't get back to me. Boy, have I got news for him.'*

I wasn't too sure if he would call me back, bearing in mind I had repeatedly tried for a job with the BBC and all I'd ever received was rejection after rejection. Surprisingly, about an hour later the phone rang. It was Nick. I simply could not hold my excitement from him and blurted out, *'I have just won a Sony Radio Award in London.'*

He immediately responded by suggesting I go and see him at Broadcasting House in Cardiff, so up to Llandaff I toddled, fags in hand. Nick said that the award was a major achievement and I felt almost as if he made up a job for me, offering me a Wednesday afternoon and Saturday breakfast show. The money was so much better than I was getting on Touch and it was also my dream job!

I called my mother and told her the Beeb had offered me a job, and asked her if I should take it. *'Yes of course you should!'* she replied, adding her line about the BBC needing a bit of class. I naturally wanted Gabe's opinion, too. All he said was one word – *'GO!'*

So, off I went, back to the Beeb, where I was given a contract, which I read and signed in the canteen – even though at the time I was still working on Touch.

It all seemed to fit together so well. My contract with Touch was just finishing and when I told them I did not wish to renew it they offered me shed loads more money to stay, but I couldn't. I had signed a contract with the BBC. I was glad that I had. I wanted to move up in the world and the Beeb was the only place to go.

About two weeks before I started I had a call from Nick asking me if I would be interested in jointly presenting a morning show five days a week. Naturally, I jumped at the chance.

The BBC was very different from Touch and it was such a new experience for me and suddenly I felt homesick for my old job and the people I used to work with. It felt better being a big fish in a small pool. God, I was nervous! Nervous? What a total understatement!

I didn't even know where the toilets were. The place was massive. It was like a city itself. Callers to the show would ring from all over Wales – I simply couldn't believe my listeners were so widespread. On Touch it was just Cardiff and surrounding areas.

I had just started on Radio Wales and to be honest I was still getting used to seeing many well-known people walking around. It was new but all sinking in slowly. I felt like a tiddler at the Beeb and looked up with amazement to others such as Owen Money and Roy Noble. I thought they were IT. I still do, to be honest.

The stint with the morning show ended and I went on to do the Wednesday afternoon and the Saturday breakfast shows. When I started the Saturday morning breakfast show I had to be bright and lively, not easy at that time of the day, and I would start off by saying, 'Good morning and welcome to BBC Radio Wales – Yo baby.' When I thought about it afterwards I was convinced I was far too jovial for that time of day.

Then a new opportunity, in the form of Radio Cymru,

opened up for me. Apparently, the editor was a very big fan of the show and thought I would be great in Welsh. God! I hadn't spoken Welsh for years. I made a few pilot programmes and they launched me big time onto the Welsh language listeners.

My picture appeared on the back of buses and on billboards across Wales. I did three-and-a-half years on Radio Cymru, and won an award for the best music programme. Sadly after this time the programme came to an end, but it was a great opportunity, which helped me improve my Welsh no end. I really enjoyed my time on Radio Cymru, and would do it all again. I thank Aled Glynne Davies and Keith Jones for the fabulous time I spent broadcasting in the Welsh language.

Come into the Garden

I still had my shows on Radio Wales. The editor, Nick, was about to leave and a new editor was to take over the running of the station. What was going to happen to me? God, was I going down the pan? Why did I leave Touch? All this a few weeks after my mother died. I was cracking up.

Nick called me into his office and sat me down. I thought, *'Oh God, what's happening here?'* He told me he was leaving and a new editor, Julie Barton, was taking his place.

I knew I had to meet her, but this was impossible as she was on maternity leave. Nick re-assured me that she was a fan of mine and she wanted me to have the late show to pull a cult audience. He told me that, although unaware of it at the time, I had already met Julie and had actually talked with her.

I started on the late show and after a few weeks I was getting a bit bored, and felt there was nothing exciting about it. It needed spicing up and I needed to come up with an idea that would do just that – something that would in effect put the show on the map and pull in the listeners.

The solution came about, more by accident than design,

while I was pondering on a few different ideas. A listener asked me one night if I had a fan club and I said, 'Yes, it's called the Garden'. *'Oh,' she said. 'I'll join.'* And then a fella said he'd like to join, too.

It seemed to be they didn't know what it was all about, but everyone had a good time and lots of people wanted to join. It was like seeing a queue of people with everyone having a smile on their faces and being happy....

CHAPTER 9

The Garden and an MBE

A human internet

I ACTUALLY STARTED THE late show on BBC Radio Wales three weeks before the Garden was launched. It wasn't planned; it was something that just happened. The full title was, *The Chris Needs Friendly Garden Association Affiliated Ltd (twice)*. Where that came from I still don't know to this day.

My first member started at number 20, though there was no-one else! Then another caller said she'd like to join the Garden, and another...the rest is now history and at the time of writing this book there are masses of people in the Garden.

Even men joined, mere males, and I remember the producer of the show, Eli Williams, daughter of the late, great Alun Williams, saying one day that there were 221 members in the Garden and that people in the BBC were starting to comment very favourably about it. We couldn't believe it!

Soon everyone within the BBC seemed to know about the Garden and the whole concept behind it. The idea was to bring listeners together as a family by re-creating a community that no longer existed, based on old fashioned ideas of value and friendship. Many listeners have built up a great friendship with other members and it is my honest belief that every member would help one another. It was all a bit strange at first, but I have to admit that I could see that this was the start of something big.

My mother's friend Val Prosser (formerly Cooper) from
Tabor, Cwmafan, was a great help to me in the early days of the
Garden. Val was great friends with my mother, and her father,
Charlie Prosser, was a big friend of my dad. Val stepped in one
day and saw the potential of the Garden and volunteered to help.
She came down my house every day to help start the Garden
book of members. She read the letters and put the names in the
book as 'mere males' and 'fab females'. She worked so hard and
I can never thank her enough for what she has done for me and
the Garden. Val still listens in to the programme. I think she
must be proud of it all. After all is said and done, she did have
something to do with it. God bless you, Val.

The Garden continued to grow. Today it's like one big extended
family living all over Wales and, thanks to the internet, across the
world.

Lots of people ask me how I'd describe the Garden and
I don't really know how to answer that. I suppose it is like
a human internet, a vast collection of knowledge and life's
experiences. If someone wants to know something, or needs a
contact for this or that, then another member will surely have
an answer and usually within minutes.

If you or your family suffer a major health issue there's
always likely to be another Garden member who has been
through a similar experience, someone who all too often can
offer great comfort and support at time when someone else's
world maybe falling apart.

When some people call I can often hear the pain in their
voice, and I know what it's like at first hand. It's awful and at
the time you feel as if it's only happening to you, I have to stress
though I am merely a FRIEND who they can turn to, as are all
the rest of the Garden members.

I've had many very varied callers on the programme,
including a doctor from Japan, Welsh people living all over

the world and lots of lonely people – this saddens me greatly, especially when people say to me, *'Chris, you are the only person I have spoken to in three days.'*

The Garden has a fair number of famous people in it as well, such as the wonderful Max Boyce, Janice Long from Radio 2, David Emanuel, PJ Proby, Katherine Jenkins, Bonnie Tyler and actors from *Pobol y Cwm*. Even BBC people are in the Garden – many of whom have been honoured with Royal titles.

Let me explain about these titles – every year honours are bestowed on deserving people, titles such as countess, lord, etc. There's the Baron of Pencoed, Dame Julie Barton, former editor of BBC Radio Wales and Sir Owen Money, to name just a few.

What started off as just a fan club has rapidly become a lifeline to many listeners. A lot of comfort has been found through the Garden, and because of this I am sent lovely letters, cards and presents. They all make me feel special and wanted.

The presents I receive are too numerous to mention, but I thank each and everyone for their kindness. To mention just a few, there's Rose from West Wales who gave me a bullet when I met her in Aberystwyth. I've had cashew nuts and olives and chocolates for Gabe from Roger and his family in Cwmdare. I've had a ton of lighters and lots of key rings, some lovely ornaments, and even a piano accordion.

Olive Blackwell regularly sends me a box of Eccles cakes or mince pies – it must cost her a small fortune, let alone the time as well. Like clockwork they turn up and I'm eternally grateful and really look forward to them. She makes the cakes sugar and fat free, so being a diabetic they really help when I want something sweet. It must cost her pounds!

The greatest gift for me however is priceless – it's the respect of the listeners. Garden members are very kind and respectful to me and to one another and I love speaking to as many as possible.

I love it when people like Dilys from Treorchy comes on the air, telling me about how she was married on Christmas Day, and says God has given me a gift. Jan and Pete from West Wales always calls me *'my happy chappy'*. I call everyone *'flower'*.

I never get fed up with the Garden. I love broadcasting and I love the boys and girls in my Garden. I really don't know what I would do without the Garden now – it's kept me in work, it's made me feel wanted, as hardly any of my own family speak to me.

The Garden has given me a purpose to get up and go to work and I thank everyone for making this possible. LONG MAY IT REIGN!

Quite an anthem

In the Garden we even have our own song. It was written by Rob Allen and myself and has turned into quite an anthem. Whenever I perform it on stage people seem to know it and everyone sings along. Everyone seems to know the words and for me that has to be a compliment.

Just in case you don't know – this is how it goes:

Chris Needs' friendly Garden is the nicest place I know
I became a member just a little while ago,
And since I've joined it's changed my life, I tell you honestly,
Chris Needs' friendly Garden is the nicest place to be...
Chorus
In the Garden, in the Garden,
That's where I meet my special friend; where fun begins and never ends,
Helping one another doing things for charity,
Chris Needs' friendly garden is the nicest place to be.

Will was in the doldrums, living on his own,
Fed up with the wet stuff, he called me on the phone.
We had a conversation, now he'll never be the same,

*He's packed his bags, he's sold his house, he's living out in
Spain.*
Chorus

*I'm really very friendly when you call me on the show,
You could learn a thing or two, or win a radio,
I'll make you feel quite welcome, I'll make you feel at home,
There's thousands in the Garden, so you'll never be alone.*
Chorus

*They're tuning in in Canada, in Spain and Bogota,
It's bouncing off the satellite, the moon and every star,
They listen in their potting sheds with spades and rakes and
trowels,
They listen when they're cwtched in bed, 'cysgwch yn dawel'!*
Chorus – *twice*

Why would the Prime Minister write to me?

As I mentioned earlier, I am merely the presenter of the show.
It's Garden members who do the rest and it is this loyal,
dedicated, band of people who listen night after night who
decided that I should be honoured for setting it up.

Never in a million years did I think that I'd get something
like a gong – I never thought for one moment I had done
anything at all to deserve it.

One day Maria, who worked in the shop, called me. She
was very excited and told me there was a letter from the
Prime Minister. I thought she was joking. Why would Prime
Minister Tony Blair write to me? Someone mischievous prank,
I thought.

So off I went to the shop in Cwmafan to see this mysterious
letter for myself. I looked closely at the envelope, and on the
outside it clearly said that it was from Downing Street.

Like a child opening a present, I hastily tore it open and
took out the contents. Inside was a letter which said that the
Prime Minister had it in mind to suggest to Her Majesty that

I should become a Member of the British Empire. Funnily enough I was not filled with immediate excitement, my initial reaction was would I still have to pay council tax?

The letter said I was not to say a word to anyone about this. Me? Chris Needs keep something like that a secret? Quite the opposite, I wanted to shout it out from the rooftops! When Maria asked me what it was all about I told her it was about my concern about VAT on gravestones and she asked no more.

Over the years I have discovered that if you answer someone by saying, 'I'm not telling you,' they only quiz you more, so I usually give an answer like that, knowing it will shut them up. Maria is a good friend who I met after my mother died. I liked her straight away, she's very much like me, and that's cool.

Knowing this news and not being able to tell anyone was driving me mental. Surely my excitement would give it away? Anyway, when it comes to keeping secrets, believe you me I can when I want to. I didn't even tell Gabe, but I think he suspected something was up. I kept going to look at the letter, reading it and re-reading it in case I had got it all wrong or misunderstood it. He must have thought at one point that I was reading a love letter from someone! Me? You know I'd rather have a good dinner.

So the weeks and the months went by and nothing more was said. I went into work on December 30th and hung around the office knowing full well that if I was to be honoured with the MBE then BBC journalists would be some of the first to hear.

I sat in the office trying to look and act cool, fumbling around in the day at a time when I was never normally around. Some asked me what I was doing in work and I remember saying that I was making a promotional trailer for my show. No-one doubted that as it sounded more than feasible. Midday came and passed with no news. Thinking the worst, that the Queen had not approved this, I packed up my things and decided to go home, sad but grateful that I had not mentioned it to anybody. I decided a strong black coffee would suffice instead.

Then, out of nowhere, a BBC journalist almost pounced on me and screamed out in front of everybody, 'Congratulations, Chris Needs MBE.' I'll let you into a secret now: media like the BBC get a copy of the list in advance, although winners' names are never revealed before the embargoed time.

So it HAD happened. My knees went from under me and I had to sit down. It had really happened. The people, my listeners, had turned up trumps. The Welsh media went to town with the news – newspapers, radio, television, were all trying to contact me.

The first person I wanted to tell was my mother, that was just a natural reaction, and I hope to this day she knows. She would have been doing cartwheels, mind. I would have had to tie her to a chair for 12 hours to preventing her telling anyone.

On with the show

No announcement could be made until one minute past midnight so like everyone else, I could not say anything for the time being. I had my show to do as usual that night – I was brimming with excitement yet I knew I had to keep my lips tightly closed for two hours. I realised I would have to say something on air during that night but would have to do two hours of the show without giving any clue. How would I cope? Would listeners guess?

I went home and switched on the computer to write the words I would say that night. Then I remembered I hadn't even told Gabe, so I phoned him on his mobile and said he was living with gentry, explaining that I had been awarded an MBE. He was so happy for me and proud.

I thought long and hard of an appropriate song to play that would convey my true feelings, and I selected 'Mama' by Il Divo.

So off I go to the studio, trying so hard to act as normal. Just before midnight I called Lewis, my assistant, into the studio and told him I had something important to say and suggested he should sit down.

He immediately thought I was leaving the show but he was so wrong. I read out my carefully prepared words. I was trembling, but I'm a brave little Cwmafan boy and managed to get to the end. This is what I said:

'I'd like to stop the show for a moment and ask Lewis to come into the studio and sit down for a minute. As we have now reached the eve of 2005 I would like to take this opportunity to say thanks to some very special people. Firstly to Lewis, Gabe, Rory and Gavin, to Mark Buckley and Howard Griffiths, Christine, Catherine and Maria at the shop for all their help throughout this year.

I would also like to thank the BBC, in particular (former) Radio Wales editor Julie Barton, head of English language programmes Clare Hudson, and Controller BBC Wales Menna Richards for such great support.

I want to say a big thank you to you, my beloved Garden. You have supported me and have been loyal to my programme, not making it big but making it colossal. Please keep on listening to the Garden show and keep joining the Garden as we are the new community in Wales, and we can put things back as they were. I thank each and every one of you from the bottom of my heart. The Garden must have worked their socks off to get the award of an MBE for me. It's something I'll never forget, and I thank them from the bottom of my heart.

I have chosen four songs to play to you which sum me up to a tee. The first song is dedicated to my mother because tonight, Garden, thanks to you, for services to broadcasting and charitable work throughout Wales... you are listening to Chris Needs MBE.'

Then I played 'Mama' and while the songs played I
went out for a fag and the security men who had heard my
announcement were chuffed. Back in the studio the telephones
went crazy. It was nothing but praise and congratulations from
every corner of the world.

Looking back, I didn't know how I felt. I was all over the
place and still had an hour of the show to finish. Somehow I
got to the end of the programme, when I have to say *'Time for
the BBC home service, BBC Radio Wales to close for another
night,'* and I started to fill up again.

I fluffed the final words at the end. I managed to say
'Cysgwch yn dawel' and then blew it. I came out with something
like *'Oh I can't do this...catch you tomorrow...God bless you all...
thank you from the bottom of my heart.'* Then I burst into tears
– again.

Hillbillies at Buck House

Let's get to the part that nearly put paid to me – meeting the
Queen.

I didn't know where to start, but thank goodness my friend
Allan Davey who had previously been honoured with an MBE
stepped in and advised me on what to do.

The BBC made a documentary of the whole day, *Chris Needs
by Royal Appointment*. It was made by Damian George and
Carwyn Jones, two ace guys who did such a professional job.

By the time the big day arrived I had nearly lost the plot.
Even before setting off I argued with Gabe, I was a wreck. Then
I heard that the Queen had caught a cold and might not be
able to do the presentation. Thank God she made a complete
recovery and did the biz for me on the day.

We were going to London in my motor home, I can still
imagine the scene – us hillbillies arriving at Buck House
and asking guards if we could link up to the electricity and
where could we empty the chemical toilet. As it happened, the

motor home didn't make it in the end. It had an oil leak which affected something on the vehicle, so we had to make a last minute change of plan.

So we went up the night before and stayed in a posh hotel, had champers in the night, and went out for a pizza, before going to bed knackered.

The morning finally came, and with it the back door gallops. I decided to go local for my suit which I bought at Oxford House in Pontycymmer. They did me proud but I couldn't do up my posh neck tie, so I threw it out of the window (some lucky so-and-so had a nice find that day). I found another and put it on.

Gabe was with me, as were Teddi Munro and Julie Barton. We took a taxi to the Palace, and for the first time I saw famous names like the Hammersmith Palais. It was all so exciting. I got out of the taxi and walked towards the Palace. I started to shake, I needed my mother with me (I'm sure she was), and we went in. I have never seen such a grand place in my life.

I was ushered off on my own to join the other lucky people who were receiving honours and my guests were taken to sit in the audience. I was shown how to address the Queen by a really entertaining chappy, and I will never forget walking past a suit of armour, and as I looked at it, I swear it blinked at me. It actually did, as there was a man inside.

The time came to get the gong. The Queen made me feel as if she really wanted to meet me and she congratulated me as she placed the medal on my lapel. She asked about my radio work, and then went on to ask, *'Do people still listen a lot to the wireless in Wales?'* I answered by saying, *'It's better than the telly, Ma'am.'* We shook hands and I limped off, as I usually do, to have my medal put in a case.

A little secret – you have a little hook put on your jacket lapel on the way in so that the Queen just has to hang the medal on it, just like hanging a towel behind the bathroom door.

Unbeknown to me, I was filmed on the way in and during the investiture, even when I was scratching my bottom. Typical Chris.

We set off for home straight away, but not before I bought a pair of London shoes. A badly placed nail in one of the soles will always remind me of my big day.

I was worn out, and by the time I reached the studio, it was all a bit too much for me. I started to have another little weep.

God bless you all!

CHAPTER 10

All in a Day's Work

Colleagues

I HAVE WORKED WITH many great radio presenters over the years. Most have been terrific but others, a right pain. There was one chap on Touch Radio in Cardiff who hated me so much that he would change all the technical settings in the studio before I went on air! I soon grew wise to this – you'll have to get up early in the morning to catch this boy. I always check everything before going live, but what made my blood boil is why did he do it? Jealousy?

I have made some wonderful friends over the years. One of my favourite presenters has to be Roy Noble. The first time I went to the BBC I saw Roy in the reception and immediately called my mother to tell her. *'Mammy, I'm stood about 10 yards away from Roy Noble,'* I said. I was overwhelmed with happiness and fear!

I find it strange that now we are good friends and if I have a problem I know I can always go to him or call him. We talk for ages on the phone; he really is a great guy. On my first day Roy gave me an acorn and said to me, 'From little acorns grow great oaks. Welcome, young Christopher.'

I think Owen Money is amazing too. How he manages to fit so much in I have no idea – panto, outside shows, television, too! I'll never know. He must be running on long-life batteries I reckon.

I love to see Owen on stage with a live audience telling jokes. I think he shines there. I would love to have a part in one of Owen's pantos, maybe as the camp cat, or Buttons, screaming around the place. That would be cool, but working five nights a week limits me a great deal.

I think Radio 2's Janice Long is a trouper. She just battles on regardless in the night and does it well. She's in The Garden and when she popped into BBC Wales while doing her show from Cardiff, we hit it off immediately. She's a dude.

It's funny, because the people we see on telly are those who I now see most days. People like Jamie Owen, Sara Edwards, Sian Lloyd, Clare Summers, Derek Brockway, Roy Noble, Owen Money, Shan Cothi, Beverley Humphreys, just to name but a few. Then there's The Tardis and the odd Dalek or two, and cyber men because of *Doctor Who*. The BBC is a great place to be.

Mind you in the early days at the BBC I wasn't quite so sure. I had to grow there, and now finally I believe that I have. I was once offered a job on another radio station, who said they were extremely interested in having me onboard, and were hoping that the Garden would follow.

Naturally I was very flattered and told this to my then boss Julie. But me being me, I simply decided, '*I ain't going. I love being a BBC boy,*' and the offer never went any further than that, I'm glad to say, as I'm very happy as things are today.

Cock-ups and close shaves

Working on the radio can reap rich rewards, like meeting members of the Garden and interesting people from all walks of life. Sometimes much happens behind the scenes that would make your hair curl, (please NO comments about my hair). People say things that have me rocking with laughter. From time to time I also get letters or comments that make me so angry. Here is a sample of the funny and unfortunate things I have experienced on air.

Once a lady called the show and asked for a Frank Sinatra song for her mother who was celebrating her 100th birthday in a nursing home. I decided to play what people would consider to be Sinatra's most famous song, 'My Way'. Unfortunately I didn't stop for a moment to consider the lyrics of this well much loved track. They went something like this, *'And now, the end is near and so I face the final curtain'*. As you see the idea was great, but that's not the sort of track you play for a 100-year-old listener. *Nice one Chris!*

In the early days of my broadcasting career I had a phone call to play a dedication for a sick lady, which I duly did, and declared the next record to her. Unfortunately it was the McGuiness Flint's 'When I'm Dead and Gone'. The moral there is to always check what record is lined up next...

Another time someone was talking to me about travelling and asked where I'd been altogether and what was my overall favourite place. Almost without thinking I said Morocco. I told her I went around the Casbah, and even had a ride on a camel. To which she replied: *'Oh I could never do that. It might toss me off.'* I spent the next 10 minutes crying helplessly on the floor.

A lady from Neyland had a go at the anagram, the competition on the radio where you have to rearrange jumbled up letters to form a word. She suggested 'rasper'. I just fell about in hysterics as my mother always used that word when my father passed wind. She'd say, 'Harold? Have you let off a rasper?'

Another caller rang the programme one night and said that her local florist had died and she felt it appropriate to have it recorded in the Garden Book of Remembrance, This is a special tribute book to remember members and loved ones who have died. Usually that means writing the deceased's name, and the names of those dear to him or her, together with the deceased's favourite song. I was told it was 'You Don't Bring Me Flowers Anymore'. Think about it!

Another night a caller came on air and asked if she could sing a little song for her deceased mother. So, feeling sorry for her, I said yes. The song went like this, *'My mother had French knickers, with buttons down the front; Every time she tootied down, you could see right up her...'* I cut her off in her prime before she could finish it and in a fluster, but in the nick of time, said, *'Time for a bit of Johnny Mathis...'*

There are so many funny incidents you simply could not make up. For example Joanie from Preston came to a benefit concert I was appearing in and won a book, *Childbirth Made Easy*. She was in her mid-70s. It never stops, does it!

There's no-one more innocent than children. Ha ha! I used to have a competition on the BBC called the *Daisy Chain* and if you answered the question correctly you would have to give another question for listeners to answer, leaving the answer with the operator in the studio. The new question was, *'What do you call a pregnant goldfish?'* The correct answer is *'a twit'*. The next thing a little girl came on the air and said, *'Nanny said twat.'* I've never coughed so loudly in my life, and simply said, *'Nak y doo...'*

There was one incident on the afternoon show when I was asked for a specific song, which I actually had on a CD. It was taken off an album and was not a specific radio edit, tracks that are usually suitable to play on air. It was NOT a record I knew well and it started off with the lyrics, *'Everything's a load of bollocks.'* Do you know, nobody said a word! I think they might have in the night. I always say that people listen more closely in the night. Phew!

Once an old lady came on air and praised me loads. She told me that she had been a widow for two years and she felt as if I was talking to her specifically, not to the crowd. Anyway she went on and on and on. I thought she was never going to end. Then came the bombshell. She said, *'I love you like nothing on earth. Well, like a mother, not like that; I know you're a homo.'* I loved it.

Another time I spoke to an elderly lady and she said she lived alone. We chatted for quite a while, then she said on air to me: 'I'd better go, my carer is here to take me off the comode.' She'd been doing a number two while talking to me!

The professional regurgitator

You meet all sorts through the radio. Once, while at Touch, a mate of mine, Jonathan, asked me if I could I put up a fella who was doing an interview for the station. I said yes straight away as I knew Jonathan very well.

The guy turned up and he really was nice. I asked him what he did and he told me he was a professional regurgitator; he swallowed things and brought them back up. I was totally unconvinced by this, so to prove it he gave us all a free show. He swallowed a goldfish and the water as well! We were all freaked out as he proceeded to throw up the goldfish and the water back into the bowl.

Next he put a Rubik's Cube in his mouth – none of the squares were in order when he swallowed it, but when he threw it back up they were all in order.

Next he swallowed sugar, drank some water then coughed up the sugar as if there had never been any water!

He kept slapping his stomach, and things just appeared, knives all sorts. It was all too much for us and nobody believed us about this guy when we told them but we saw it with our own eyes. Freaky or what? A few months later, he was on Channel 4. I screamed at Gabe, but he wasn't around when this guy had stayed with me. It was something I'll never forget, though. Incredible!

You can't please them all

As well as the good, there are the bad and the ugly. You would never believe the number of nasty letters from listeners saying things like, 'You shouldn't be allowed a godson; you'll probably turn him into a queer like you. Then others, like, 'People of your sexual orientation should be burned and you should hand back the MBE.'

I had a letter from a person in the Rhondda saying that I'm a right bragger, talking all the time about my boat in Cardiff Bay. She went on to say that it was alright for me, but some people in the Valleys were on the bones of their arses. She forgot I was brought up with a similar Valleys lifestyle and I'm stronger for it – that I was determined to make something of my life. I believe if you work hard enough you can have achieve almost anything you want. My success didn't come out of a Christmas cracker. I worked damn hard for it and if I want anything I'll bloody well work for it.

I get a lot of sad, lonely, drunk women calling the show. It's impossible to get through to many of them as they are firmly stuck in a lonely, judgmental world, and drink is their only escape. They claim to know best, so I just let them get on with it and feel sorry for them. They must be neglected. Pity.

At the end of the day I'm only paid to put records on, but I've managed to turn the show into something bigger with a character of its own. I will always try to put something back into the community if I can and if you don't like what I do on the radio then you can switch over like you do the telly – but thank God lots do like me!

If you don't have the guts to say who you are, then stop writing anonymous letters. To be honest I laugh at most of them. If the show does not appeal to you, do something else – don't write in. It will save you a lot of time, paper and postage costs and give you more time to wash your nets!

The Government can turn around and say that petrol is

going up, as is road tax; that you have to wear a seat belt or can't use a mobile phone in the car and you can't smoke in any public place, yet all some people want to do is to mouth on about is me.

Success, they say, doesn't come on its own. All my life I have strived to become famous. Sadly now I have it I'm not fussed on it.

I was called one night by a lady in Carmarthen. She said I was selfish and only concerned about myself and that I was 'taking the mick' out of diabetics. Being a diabetic myself I was furious and I went ape and put her right. I really do believe that there are a certain amount of people just sat there looking for something to complain about.

I'd rather devote my energies to fundraising work and my chapel than argue with sad people who are so entrenched in their own miserable world. Such people used to really annoy and anger me, but now I see them for what they really are, simply a waste of space.

I can sleep at night. I'm not ashamed of being me. I'm just another human being who happens to love another human being. For the first time in my life I am proud of myself and what I have achieved, not only with the Garden but with life in general.

It's been a long difficult passage for me but even now I still ask myself, what have I done to deserve this honour? I don't know, but one thing I am happy about is that it came from the people. I have always tried to please. My listeners, the Garden... this family always comes first and will every time.

On the telly

I love doing telly, too. The BBC made a programme on me called *The Chris Needs Experience*, based on the success of the Garden. It was a fab programme, and I felt so good having done it. It was a great compliment.

Then I made another programme called *Chris Needs Lightly Grilled*, which featured an audience asking various questions. It was another good one and in the audience was my friend Christine from Willington, who wanted to know why I never married. I answered by saying, *'Well, Gabe hasn't asked me yet,'* which brought the house down.

Gillian Elisa asked me would I ever consider joining the Forces. I told her that I went for an interview with the army and this chap asked me, *'Chris, do you think you could kill a man?'* After a while I said, *'Eventually, love; eventually.'* That was a stunning show.

Anything that makes you laugh has to be worth it. I've since done a few others like *Pobol y Cwm*, *High Hopes*, and a few others such as the Eisteddfod and *The Lyric Game* with Mike Doyle.

CHAPTER 11

Life at South Fork

Home sweet home

I HAVE SEVERAL HOUSES, some left to me, and some I've just moved on from for security reasons. I have never sold any as I cannot bear to be parted from them. I know they are only possessions but they are like family to me. I am a hoarder too, and keep ridiculous things like bus tickets from 1972.

Where I live now is just outside Porthcawl and we moved there through desperation. Fame doesn't come alone. I was driven out of my home in Cardiff. What with my car being vandalised several times a month and the daubing of my mother's house and grave, I simply couldn't live in Cwmafan or Cardiff any longer.

So I now live out in the sticks, where I don't even have to lock my car anymore and I don't have to put up with stupid, jealous people. (The funny thing about this situation is that none of this ever happens to me in Spain, Jersey or France. Only here in Wales.) By accident I discovered the perfect house and said to Gabe, 'Pack! We're moving.' Gabe being Gabe went along with it to keep me happy.

I call this house South Fork, as in *Dallas*. It has a lot of grounds, is very private and has a drive where you can park loads of cars. The house is completely detached from anything and anyone. It's a listed building and has a spiral staircase leading up to the bedrooms with a trap door. Good job I don't drink!

The bar in the lounge makes my house look like a country club, which pleases me no end as my whole life has centred around clubs. I could live in a disco. The bar has just about every drink you can imagine, and the lounge has a grand piano, a 50-inch television, a fireplace right up to the ceiling and a log burner. The French doors open on to acres of ground and I've bought a sit-down lawn mower.

The dining room is really big, with an extremely long table, another widescreen television and a piano. I also have a lot of leather furniture and Spanish wood items as well. The utility room has an ice machine – guests love that – and all bedrooms are en-suite.

A lot of my stuff comes from Spain, with its rich dark wood. Although, having said that, I do have a large Chesterfield settee and a captain's chair. Often, on the spur of the moment, I go abroad in my motor home and come back laden with porcelain, ornaments or wall hangings.

I'm desperate for a housekeeper, but it's all a trust issue for me. I wouldn't want anyone telling others they work for Chris Needs. So I get on with the cleaning myself. I find it quite hard not having help around the house. I can't get a good cleaner for love nor money. Everyone I've had has either let me down, pinched things from me or told tales about me. The only good one I had was Maureen, my dear friend who was so faithful. Sadly she is no longer with us.

I spend a lot of my time alone in this big isolated house. I reckon I could hold a pop festival here and nobody would even hear it. However, I DO want to move back to Cardiff – I didn't think I would miss it so much. This is great, but simply far too quiet for me. I would have moved by now had it not been for my godson, Sammy, who has kept me here as I love to see him as much as I can.

I do miss Cardiff – the shops, the people, the closeness to the studio and my friends in the city. Cardiff is so special for me.

It's my home. I hope I don't upset anyone by being honest, but I never felt that I had a home until I lived in Spain. I felt the same when I lived in Cardiff. The people there are so special. Maybe it's because I am biased as Gabe is a Cardiffian, but as a Valleys boy myself, Welsh speaking and with other languages, I feel so comfortable in Cardiff. It is so cosmopolitan.

I dearly love Cardiff people, especially those from areas like Splott and Grangetown. Over the years I have met a lot of characters, such as Barry Brading and the boxer David 'Darky' Hughes, a tremendous guy. I made so many friends at the Grange and Riverside Labour clubs; nice people who have supported me in everything I've done. They affectionately called me Gloria as in Gloria Hunniford and I loved it.

A day in the life

Many people think I live an exciting life – I don't think so – but please judge for yourself.

I get in from the studio at just after two in the morning and have a Spanish coffee. I then go up to see Gabe and wake him to say, 'I'm back' and ask if he's alright. He usually grunts something undecipherable and promptly goes back to sleep.

I go downstairs and switch the telly on and there's *The Weakest Link*. I love Anne Robinson. I've got Sky and Hot Bird, a European satellite. I love the Dutch channel and watch Spanish soaps and Dutch game shows. I watch a few programmes recorded from the night before, and usually go to bed about 4am. I get up and, if I haven't done them the night before, I make Gabe his sandwiches for lunch then I take my diabetic tablet, and the day starts again.

I usually empty the dishwasher and watch out for the postman, Mike. He's a nice guy and I often call him in for coffee and a chat. I then go through the mail and open the curtains, that's a big job. Boy, have I got big windows. My music goes on, I have a jukebox and I usually play Il Divo or something Spanish. All too often I look out the window and see nothing but cloud and sigh for the continent and the sun. After a couple of strong black espressos I wash and dress, choose a cap to wear to hide my horrible hair and head for the shops.

I love shopping, it's my favourite sport. If I was snowed in the house for six months, and the army had to dig me out, the first thing I would ask them is, 'Do you want to borrow anything, boys?' I buy tins of diet cola by the 100 and bread galore. I have six freezers – and they are all full! I buy lots of olives and usually have them around breakfast time or to take to the studio to nibble on at night. Mmm, lovely!

A local pub (The Farmer's, St Brides, or the pub on the pond) has welcomed me with open arms and when I walk in the first thing they enquire about is whether I've eaten. They usually then produce something like chicken drumsticks and chips from the kitchen. They worry about my diabetes and look after me so well. They are such nice people.

The Baker's Boy café in Porthcawl, near the police station, is wonderful. I go to the café, order my breakfast, then usually to the bank, where the people are so wonderful to me. I never have to fill out a paying in slip, they always do it for me, fair play to them. Then it's back to The Baker's Boy for my tailor-made grub, a feast fit for a king I might add.

On the way I meet lots of people who listen to the programme and I love saying hello to them. Some are too embarrassed to speak, but I really don't mind if they want to, it's a compliment.

Usually I then go to supermarket opposite, which sells the best bread I have ever tasted. Then it's off to the chemist (for a change!) before returning home – not forgetting to pop over and check my caravan in Trecco Bay for electricity, etc.

After getting home I have lots of paperwork to do and calls to make before settling down for an afternoon nap! Every day I have a siesta – too long in Spain, love! Each tea time I go to bed for a few hours, getting up in time to ensure Gabe and I have a cooked tea.

I leave South Fork at about 8.30 and get to the Beeb for nine-ish, set my studio up ready for the show and put my sandwiches and pop out ready to eat. I try to eat the noisy things like crisps before I go on air and leave the olives for when I'm having a chat, as they don't make so much noise.

Not many listeners realise I am munching away on silent olives or trying to conceal the noisy stuff for when the records are on. My mother used to say, 'You eat two shovel-fulls more than a pig. In fact, the pig would have given up years ago.'

As I've already mentioned I speak to many people on the radio who have been through terrible times, for example the loss of a partner or child or a parent. I speak as best I can on air to them and usually end up phoning them back after one o' clock after Radio Wales closes down. I drive home and when I get there I lie in bed thinking about them. I have been in such tatters in my time and know what it's like. I eventually drop off and wake up a couple of hours later and then it's time to make sandwiches for Gabe's lunch....

Willy and Delyth Du

You could lose your granny around my house in Porthcawl because it's so big. There is a lot of open countryside. I'm surrounded by wild animals, including pheasants, rabbits, hawks, wood pigeons and robins. Some of these are cheeky and even venture into the house. There's Brenda the pigeon and Audrey and Ron the pheasants. Audrey hates Ron, though they always appear together. If Ron tries to get his wing over she batters the poor dab.

In the 80s I had two cats. Willy and Delyth Du. Willy was old and cuddly but Delyth Du was a little black cat, and was a wild one.

One day my friend Maureen – she was a listener to my Touch AM show and we became great friends, she's almost like a sister to me – decided to go to the animal shelter in Cardiff to drop some food off. While we were there, this black and white cat jumped into my arms and started purring. We laughed and I said, 'I've just given birth to a boy!' I shouldn't have laughed as I had that cat for about 10 years. He was 15 when I had him. I named him Willy and everyone loved him.

My mother would only speak Welsh to him and he would only react if you talked in Welsh. If my mother said, 'Willy, food,' he would just do nothing. But if she said, 'Willy, *bwyd*,' he'd come running.

His favourite food was melted ice cream and one day I left a half-eaten onion on the kitchen table to kill any germs that were lurking about. (I know, an old wives' tale) and when I got up in the morning Willy had eaten it all!

The other listeners on Touch AM would say, 'How's that Willy of yours?' and I always replied, 'Marvellous, he was out first thing this morning chasing birds.' Boy, did I get some mileage out of that cat.

Delyth Du was named after the Welsh actress Delyth Wyn. Delyth Du teased poor old Willy terribly when she was on heat. Mind you, he had a right good go, love him. I would tell the two of them, 'I keep a respectable house here. I'll not have this nonsense on my stairs, thank you very much.' They never listened.

One summer's evening I was in bed with the window open when a seagull flew in and landed on the bed. Delyth Du was asleep in the corner of the room but I was petrified and peeped out from under the bed clothes at this monster of a bird. I sort of whispered and shouted at the same time to the cat,

'Delyth, get him, go on, girl, get him,' and by damn she did. She went for the seagull's throat and they fought for about a minute until the bird did a runner. My cat had saved me. Boy oh boy, did she get a reward. Tuna in brine. That's my girl.

While all this was going on Willy was half asleep and probably totally unaware of all the fuss.

On one occasion when I lived in Cardiff Bay, Willy, who by this time was quite blind, tried to chase birds perched on top of a shed, but the poor thing fell off and broke his two front legs. The vet told me that he probably wouldn't survive. He set the legs in plaster and told me to watch him, but reckoned Willy would die. The operation cost me over £400. I paid it. Who wouldn't?

Someone asked me why the bloody hell did I waste such a large amount of money on a lousy old cat, an animal that didn't have long on this earth? What a nasty thing to say. I replied by singing. *'I'll never let you go – why because I love you!'* – the Tony Newley song. I know I'm insane but at the same time I'm not God. He's the one that gives and takes, not me!

They were great company. Gabe never knew Delyth Du. He arrived shortly after she disappeared. Willy died just after my mother died. After that I decided that was it as far as pets were concerned, as work commitments meant it was not right or fair to leave them alone for such long hours. I think that may have been just an excuse. To be honest, I was fed up of cleaning up after them. Not a nice job.

Another cat we had was Gaynor. There's not a lot to say about Gaynor really. She was a mink-coloured kitten, the daughter of Delyth Du. I named her after Bonnie Tyler. I don't like names like Tiddles and Fluffy – Willy, Gaynor and Delyth Du seemed right to me. I always remember a TV producer coming to see me in my Cardiff apartment (sorry, flat) and I had to impress him big time. As soon as he sat down Willy sat in the litter tray, lifted his tail and farted. The producer had to have a drink of water as he was crying so much with laughter. The fart was like a piano concerto – I thought it would never end.

Smoking

Since the age of nine I have smoked, and smoked like a trooper. I used to pinch my father's Woodbines while he was asleep and he would blame my mother. It was so trendy to smoke back in the 70s and especially with the high-flying job I had, rushing everywhere. I never smoked British cigs, only Spanish ones, and any brand that resembled a Camel. I worked for years in Spain and I never paid for a drink or a fag. I would tank up on the fags when I was returning home as all of my family smoked. I have often tried to give up the fags, but it was not to be, I was totally addicted to the weed and I found a lot of comfort smoking them as well. I couldn't walk to the post box without taking a full packet of cigarettes with me and two lighters in case the flint went. I never went on any long hauls abroad as I couldn't go without a fag for that long.

One Wednesday night while I was on air, my tongue began to swell and I was talking as if I had a gobstopper in my mouth. Paul Needs was on the phones that night and he suggested that I went to the hospital on the way home, which I did. The doctor told me that I had an allergic reaction to something or other and put me on a drip. A few hours later I was feeling much better and went home. Paul and his wife Beth both agreed that I should just go to bed, and I did. Gabe was away, so I did what I was told and went straight to have some sleep.

I lit a fag but had to put it out, then I lit another the following day, but couldn't smoke it. I began to cough badly, but I had the craving for a fag, so I ate a pickled onion, and the craving went away. I did this for the first day, and after that I never had a craving again. It's years now since I smoked, in fact I can't remember smoking. It can be done – I was on 100 a day, and the day my mother died I smoked 225 fags.

If I can do it… anyone can!

Think about this. I used no gums or patches – it's not hard to give up smoking, it's the thought of it that's hard, honestly! There was a time that I would have chained myself to railings over smokers' rights, but now I just try and encourage people to try and give up. I never realised how bad it is for your health.

Driving in my car

I like to go out in my cars every day. They are like my children to me. My love of cars was something I inherited from, guess who, yes, my mother. She was totally hooked on them and knew everything about motors.

Our first car was a Hillman Minx, it was red and cream. I remember when I was only about six or seven years old sitting in the back when we were involved in a road accident. Apparently another car had collided with us, although all I recall is the car shaking. I remember my father was shouting at some fella. While this was going on my mother sat me on a garden wall. I looked at the car and it was a sorry mess and I started to cry. I recall a lovely lady consoling me and trying to stop the tears. It was a long time before the car was on the road again. One day I arrived home from school and saw the Hillman restored to its former glory in the back lane. My mother and father were beaming with joy and I felt as if a family member had just come out of hospital.

After that we had a Vauxhall, a big green one, I thought it looked a bit American. It had leather bench seats and a gear stick on the column. One day I was in the front of the car, when my mother, who was driving, suddenly screamed out loud and slammed the brakes on. The steering wheel had come off in her hands. (I don't think I'd better say what she said, but I recall it sounded a bit Russian. Well, it ended in 'off' anyway!)

When I was 15, my father bought a Honda 50 bike to nip around on. It was fantastic and I wanted it. I was too young to ride it myself but I did have a sly go every so often on some private land owned by my father's friend. I soon got the hang of it and when the day came for me have a licence and ride it out on the road, it was a day I'll never forget. I jumped on, and off I went up towards Pwll-y-Glaw. It was the first time I'd ridden on a highway and I felt good and free.

I was now 16 with my own L plates. I put in for my test, and the date came back. So I got up early on the day of the test and thought I would check the oil to make sure everything was okay. My father was in work, and I did something that caused half the engine to fall off. I was devastated, the bike would not start. My father came home from work and I won't tell you what he called me, but he tried his best. He eventually did manage to get it running but I got to the test too late. I should have stuck to playing the piano that day and left the poor bike alone.

I had a lot of pleasure out of that bike. I used to pop down and see my aunties, Hilary and Betty, and I even went up the Rhondda to Porth to see my Aunty Ann, stopping at every phone box to tell my mother that I was alright. I would say, *'Mammy, I'm in Cymer.'* I had to call her every time I saw a phone box.

I drove to THAT school in Port Talbot on my nifty 50. It gave me freedom and I loved every second of it.

My first car was an orange Mini. I was playing keyboards in Swansea and was traipsing back and forth in that car like a right go-getter. One day a friend of mine, Alison, jumped in and we went over to my father's allotment in Baglan. I parked the car on some grass, and it rained so much the car sank into the ground. It looked like the car was only 18 inches tall by the time the rained stopped. My father bailed me out of that one again.

The real posh cars came into our lives when my mother opened the shop in 1972 at the same time as I started in the Townsman Club in Swansea, now called Barrons.

No more vans or Ford Escorts for us, she would say. We'd hit the big time and had a Jaguar each. My mother's was lilac; mine was pink and was called the Pink Panther. I loved it.

People in Cwmafan stopped and stared at me – I loved being different and hated to be normal.

I think I had about 14 cars in about six years – all down to my mother of course. 'You might be dead a week on Wednesday,' she would say to me. She always wanted a convertible or, as she would say, a car with a lid. She was such a poser, what with her suede coats and the gold and the cars. I wonder where I get it from?

Caravans are brill

One day I went down to visit some friends called 'the Dirty Dogs' down Trecco Bay. They are two great lads, also Garden members, and I was talking to them when I decided to have a look at some caravans with a driveway, some ground around them, and of course security.

I was looking at this new caravan when a chap came up to me and asked me if I was that fellow on the wireless. He suggested I should nip around the corner to see his family, so I did. I went into this lovely caravan, in fact it was more like a bungalow. They asked if I was interested in buying a caravan and I said yes. They then went on to explain they were selling theirs and at a reasonable price. I was over the moon and bought it there and then. But the uncanny thing about this sale was the name of the woman – wait for it, Margaret Rose, the same name as my mother.

Gabe and I have had great times down the caravan; it has a drive and a garden. Just what the doctor ordered. I have since upgraded it, it's like a luxury home and I often have some of my friends to stay. It's also a great place for me to hide in and do some serious work.

When I sit in the caravan I could be anywhere. I know I'm a lucky guy to have such things, but I work hard for everything. I never take much time off, and I always try to do a bit for charity, and the odd hospital visit.

I let a lot of people stay at my mobile home as I don't like people staying in my house, as I like to walk around in my shorts. Not a pretty sight!

I have made a lot of great chums down Trecco Bay, and I thank them for looking after me and the home while I'm away. Caravans are brill!

A life on the ocean wave

I've always loved the sea and being a Pisces this next bit is quite fitting. My dear friend Teddi Munro has had a boat for donkeys' years. I'd always fancied one myself and, yes, you've guessed it, I could live on one. So I went and looked at a few and finally decided on an American speed boat. It has a double bedroom and a toilet and I fell in love with it the moment I saw it in Swansea.

You don't need to have any qualifications to sail a boat, which seems a bit daft to me as there are no lay-bys out at sea if you come a cropper. Gabe found this out one day when he got stuck in Cardiff Bay with the propeller twisted around a buoy. The rescue people had to come and free us. Men...I don't know!

I passed my boat licence at the same time as Teddi as we did it together. I can go out to sea on my own and in fact part of this book was written in the Bristol Channel, which is one of the most dangerous tides in the world. Trust us to have that!

I've been sailing at great speeds, tossing up and down on the water like a stone skimming the surface. Once I went out through the barrage when the tide was low and I could see fish lying on the sand. I felt I should be in a Jeep not a boat.

I went out a few hundred yards and I could still see the bottom of the sea. You have to be very careful in the Bristol Channel as it has shifting sands, which means the sea bed is constantly on the move. It's always advisable to have what is called a fish finder, which shows you how deep the water is, or if there is shallow water ahead.

Peggy, Gabe's mam came out around the bay and out to sea with us one day and she sat there singing 'A Life on the Ocean Wave' while trying to put lipstick on. You need calm weather to get the best out of the boat, and as usual in Wales, weather tends to ruin everything.

I like to get on the boat in the afternoon and I often fall asleep onboard. I sleep like a baby. It's the rocking of the water that sends me to sleep big time.

Showbusiness: Teddi Munro (top right); with Stan Stennett and Mandy Starr (bottom).

Me in Guernsey. I love the Channel Islands.

My mother had a grandson – Willy the cat.

My mother (3rd from left) and the girls in Jersey. Christine, my friend from County Durham, on the far left.

No chips on my shoulder!

'All the nice boys love a sailor!'

With former mayor John Rogers JP.

Mayor for a minute. I love a bit of bling bling!

Me and my friend, author Jack Higgins.

Me and Lisa Barsi.

Friends of the George Thomas Hospice. On the right – Iris Williams, George Thomas and Allan Davey.

Me, Joan Regan, Ronnie Hilton, and Ruby Murray.

Behind the bar with Uncle Gabe.

Gabe.

Teddi, Paul, me, Holly Holyoake, Bruce, Jan-Ross and dancers.

Il Divo and me.

My godson shows me how to play the piano.

Sam looking for his camel.

Sam supporting Liverpool.

Under starter's orders – the British Heart Foundation Walk for Life.

Left: Opening new Samaritans in Bridgend.

Below: Bruce, Mandy, Mal Pope, Nina Dusky and me.

Above: Bonnie Tyler and me on a friend's wedding day.
Below left: Tressie – Angie from Gibraltar.
Below right: With Li Harding, opening Harry's Hotel/Restaurant in
Aberystwyth.

*A good turn-out from the Garden members
at Swansea's Food Festival.*

Above: me at home, relaxing.

Below: me, Peggy and the Cameron family.

Above: me and Gillian Elisa on a good day.
Above right: Elaine and Roy Noble OBE.
Below: with Gillian Elisa, David Emanuel, Mick, Gwenda Owen and Emlyn.

Opposite page:
Bottom left: with Frank Hennessy and Hywel Gwynfryn.
Bottom right: me and cow in Stan's Stennett's pantomime, Jack and the Beanstalk. Spot the cow!

I love you all!

The Network
Chris Needs, Frank Hennessy, Hywel Gwynfryn
BBC CYMRU WALES

*A day I'll never forget.
Below: with former BBC
Radio Wales editor Julie
Barton, Gabe, and family
friend Teddi Munro.*

CHAPTER 12

Friends

Bruce, Claire and Sam

THERE ARE VERY FEW people who I can say are really close to
me. As for friends in school, I don't think I had any true friends,
just people who were sometimes nice and sometimes not.
However there are three people who are very dear to me – my
mother, Gabe, and, of course, Sammy.

As you can imagine, I get loads of email every day and
believe it or not, I actually read every one. On one occasion a
particular note caught my attention, I am not sure why, but
it did. It was from a singer called Bruce Anderson, asking me
about my music. He was a regular listener to my show on BBC
Radio Wales and somewhat of a musician himself. From what
I could gather, he sounded like he was midway from being in
a boy band to being a more mature male singer. There was
something about this email – I don't know what, something
intrigued me, urging me to find out more.

Bruce mentioned that I might know his mother, Jan Ross,
but the name didn't ring any bells. I met Bruce at a petrol
station and he came back to the house for a cuppa and to play
his CD. He was impressed with my grand piano, my studio,
a million CDs, the jukebox, bar, etc. He then played me a
recording of his voice and after eight bars I recognised the
great talent he possessed. I melted! What an incredible voice
this boy had.

His voice gave me the shivers. I'm always looking for good

Welsh talent to play on the radio and in live shows, such as Katherine Jenkins, Dame Mandy Starr and Phillip Aaron, so Bruce and I became good buddies.

On one occasion we unexpectedly bumped into one another at a social club in Aberafan. I had been invited to receive an award from the people of Port Talbot and, unknown to me at the time, Bruce was there receiving a trophy for Welsh Vocalist of the Year. During the hustle and bustle of the event I met his wife and his mam, but it was just a fleeting glance and still her name didn't click as I was rushing through the door to get to the studio in time.

I offered Bruce a chance to sing on my show at the Swansea Grand, *Chris Needs and Friends*, a big occasion and a great opportunity for Bruce. Mandy was also on the bill and she and Bruce sang a duet. It was Freddie Mercury and Monserrat Caballe's 'Barcelona'. They were a match made in heaven.

Bruce and Mandy became a regular part of the show and the three of us would rehearse at home with me on the piano. Every so often Bruce would bring his baby son, Sam, along too. I suppose the baby was between six and eight months old at the time.

On the first occasion I met Sam it was like something unexplainable happened. The little baby smiled at me and that was it. I was smitten with him. As time went by Sam got to know me. One day he said, 'Chris', and I nearly cried. He would run to me and hug me and say, 'I love you, Chris.' Boy, did he know what buttons to push.

I have his laugh on my mobile phone and I play it quite often when I feel a bit down. I get asked to play his laughter when I visit hospitals and often, too, when I'm on the radio.

One day I held a very exclusive party in the grounds of my house, with a buffet, superb music and, thank God, the weather was brilliant. Sam loves the open air and ran up and down the grass for hours. We played games and I taught him some

Welsh. He would laugh and hug me and then Gabe. It was all so wonderful. Then they popped the question: Bruce and his wife Claire asked me to be Sam's godfather, and I nearly fell through the floor.

At first I didn't know what to say, or how to react, and wanted to think about it carefully. Was it right for someone like me to have a godchild? Would I be the right kind of influence on him? It was abundantly clear that Sam loved me very much indeed, and Bruce and Claire really wanted me to accept, so I said yes and sobbed with joy.

I give the youngster a lot of material things – that's my way, but if I offered him a million pounds it wouldn't cover the love I have for him. To me Sam is my child, the child I never had, someone I would die for. That little boy has taught me how to live and love again and he is so special to me.

I have to thank Bruce and Claire for sharing him. I now baby-sit and look after him and I cherish every moment we spend together.

Let me tell you about Jan Ross, Bruce's mam. While we were doing a show one night Jan was in the reception when I accidentally bumped into her. I said, 'Jan, what the hell are you doing here?' I knew she lived in London and seeing her again was quite a shock.

'I'm here to see my son,' she replied. 'Is he in the audience?' I asked her. 'No, he's standing by the side of you.' It was Bruce. I nearly died. I remember Jan carrying him before he was born when she and I were great buddies in the 1970s. She would sing and I'd accompany her on keyboards. What a small world! Bruce had said I knew his mam – but until now it had just not clicked!

Sam always knows to come to me when he wants something like a biscuit or sweets. One day his dad had said for me not to give him any more biscuits as they are too sweet for him – so when Sam sneaked into the kitchen, remember he is still under the age of two, and asks in a whisper if he can have one, what am I supposed to do? Naturally, I always say no – at first, but he always winks at me, saying, 'Don't tell Dad!'

He's started playschool once a week and we've all been on tenterhooks counting the minutes until it's time to pick him up. He's definitely a resilient little boy and mixes well. I certainly hope his schooldays are better than mine.

Bruce and Claire have made an old Welsh man very, very happy indeed.

Teddi, Mandy and Mal

True friends are very few and far between. By the word 'friend' I mean someone that has earned the title over decades. To me, a friend is someone you know is not going to stop speaking to you tomorrow. There have been quite a few so-called friends who, if I didn't call them, I'd never hear from until they wanted something like show tickets or a record played on air.

To this day I remain great friends with Teddi Munro, the singer/comedienne from Cardiff. We met on a television programme back in 1978 and we are still like brother and sister. She is a trustee of the hospital appeal (more of which later). I recently treated her to a trip to Berlin as a thank you for always being there for me. She was so shocked by this and loved every moment of the trip.

Teddi is one of the most talented ladies I have ever met, and as long as the Lord and the audience want us, we'll carry on regardless.

Dame Mandy Starr should be singing in La Scala in Milan. Her voice is like an angel and she has proved over and over that she is nothing but a pure, true friend and I love her very much. I met Mandy in a club in the Valleys and we hit it straight off. She was singing pop songs and ballads and did really well. In the dressing room she started singing opera, and I couldn't believe what I heard, she was incredible. I told her straight away that she had to pursue this type of music, which she did with the help of my theatre shows. She is now riding so high in the opera world that I'm chuffed. She has sung at the Millennium Stadium, and in massive venues all over the UK and has made some wonderful albums. Long may she reign, and may she never stop singing.

Mal Pope has to be one of the greatest modern day musicians/songwriters/singers I have ever met. He has helped me no end.

When I wanted to write a new song for the Garden I went to Mal to get some help. While I was in his studio he told me all about the musical he was writing called *The Contender*, the life story of boxer Tommy Farr. He played some of the tracks and asked me to sing along to one of the songs. So I did and it suited me and Mal asked me to perform it in the actual show and on the CD too! I only went out for a tin of peas, and there I was in a musical. Only for quarter of an hour, but it was my 15 minutes of fame. Hey, let's rock and roll, that's what I say.

The rehearsals were very strange as the other cast members were doing just about everything and there was I sat in the corner waiting to be called for my short spot. I sat and watched the performance and discovered that what I thought of Mal had escalated one hundred fold. I came to the conclusion that he was a genius. As I watched the acting, and listened to the singing, I began to weep. It was so beautiful, and Mal just sat there playing the piano. For Mal, it must have been like watching a child growing up into to a great big star seeing his dream become a reality.

I had to be choreographed and learn lots of movements for my short appearance, but like always they were changed several times – bits cut out, and put back in – but it all came together well in the end. I would love to do more work with Mal; maybe he should do *Chris Needs – The Musical*. (Who the hell would want to play me? Answers on the back of a postage stamp, please.)

When I work on radio or live on stage I am usually the one who is always in control, but now I was told everything I had to do, and believe me this was a new experience. To work on stage with Peter Karrie was something else. I've renamed him Gentleman Pete, a true description, and a pleasure to know.

As for Mike Doyle, what the audience didn't know is that backstage all he did was impersonate me, and bloody well I must add. He would come up to me and say, 'Are you in the Garden, flower? Never!' Apparently he's put me in his act on stage. What a tribute. Mind, he worries me a bit – he does me better than I do!

I was in *Aladdin* with Anne Aston and Ivor Emmanuel way back in the 70s. I'm glad to say that I have met Ivor, and what a wonderful guy he was. At one point I played the genie of the ring – more nice clothes to wear! I also played one of the brothers in *Joseph and the Amazing Technicolor Dreamcoat*. I'm sure it was the clobber that drew me to the stage all those years ago. But I was on the up and up and nothing was going to stop me. I was game for anything that came along.

And then there was Shirley Bassey. I have always loved Dame Shirl, and one day, thanks to my friend Allan Davey, I received a call from her management in London asking me to be one of the supports on her live concert in Cardiff Castle.

This was a big thing for me to do, but I did it. I had a stretch limo to take me there and I got to meet La Bassey, and heard her rehearsing as well. I stood up in front of 10,000 people and did pretty good. I was also on stage with the Bootleg Beatles. This show I will never forget – I can see my mother now sat in front row, beaming with joy. We all left the castle in the big stretch limo and stopped for fish and chips on the way home.

Countess Christine and Lady Kathryn

No chapter on friends would be complete without a mention of the wonderful Christine. Quite simply, there would be no charity shop without Countess Christine and her daughter, Lady Kathryn, who work relentlessly. I wouldn't know where to start if I didn't have these two fabulous ladies by my side.

It all started when Christine wrote to me just after her husband Alan died. She needed to have a bit of meaning back in her life. After my mother's death I didn't want to continue with a sweet/grocery shop. It was simply too much. But today the two shops, now charity shops, are ticking over just fine with the help of my two wonderful volunteers. There's no date on any stock to worry about, and the shops are a great drop-in centre for all types of people, who want to meet for a chat and where Garden member can meet other Garden members. I love meeting Garden members and it's an excuse to go out for the afternoon. You never know who you'll meet down the shops!

It's not easy keeping things going sometimes. We've had days, believe you me, when we've only taken 65p, but I try and keep thing going by doing a couple of shows. It would be sad if the shops closed, there's a bit of history there.

So, not only have Countess Christine and Lady Kathryn become terrific charity volunteers but they have become great friends. Kathryn is like a niece or a god daughter and Christine the sister I never had. I wouldn't know where to start if I didn't have these two fabulous ladies by my side.

They now know me so well they get things done before I even ask. They sell all the goods for the charity in the shop or out at gigs, empty all the boxes on the bars in clubs and pubs, and bank all the cash. I am blessed with their friendship and would be destroyed if I never saw them again. I trust them so much and that's a rare thing these days. I've told Christine secrets, many secrets about me. I know they would go no further.

I phone Christine nearly every night on the way home from work and we have a good natter. We put the world to rights. I wish her every happiness with her life and the same to Kathryn. They are two very important ladies in my life.

Gaynor, aka Shereen, aka Bonnie

I'd never met anyone of consequence until the 1970s. At the time I played with a band called Imagination, we used to play in Swansea's Townsman Club. And my first claim to fame of knowing someone famous just happened to be one of our band – though I didn't know it at the time.

The band consisted of Gaynor on vocals, she had a remarkable voice; there was also bass player Kevin, Mike on guitar; a drummer called Rob and yours truly on keyboards. One day when I turned up for rehearsal an excited Kev stopped me and calmly said that we were going on ITV's *New Faces*.

Wow! I had never done television before and this was something, well something else. The big day arrived and we set off excitedly and nervously for Birmingham. We stopped in the Holiday Inn, right next to the ATV studios.

After a wash and change of clothes we headed for the studio and in we went. The first person we met was show host Derek Hobson. It was all so very exciting. He was bigger than I thought. I'd only ever seen him on a small screen in the corner of our room and here I was standing next to one of the most famous people I had ever met at the time.

The Saturday night show was cult viewing, a 1970s version of *Pop Idol* or *The X Factor* where bands and singers were discovered, or more often than not, humiliated on national television.

Our chosen track was called 'Armed and Extremely Dangerous' and we were going to be judged on our performance by Tony Hatch, Mickey Most, Clifford Davies and Arthur Askey. We came fourth and I remember one of the comments to this day from Mickey Most. 'There's something about the girl's voice, she could have a hit record,' he said. How right he was to be.

So that was our television debut – our one and only performance, a moment of glory over and gone forever. Not long afterwards I remember Gaynor telling me that her new manager wanted to change her name. At the time she was known as Shereen Davies, but they wanted to call her something they thought was more commercial – Bonnie Tyler. I thought that sounded like a Scottish roofer, but change it she did, and look what happened.

Gaynor, aka, Shereen, now known as Bonnie Tyler, went on to do some fabulous tracks and in 1976 blasted into the charts with 'Lost in France', closely followed by other tracks such as 'Total Eclipse of the Heart'. I was so very happy for her and as she swapped her Swansea nightclub for a world stage I went on to do my bits abroad – and loved it.

The Viscount and Iris

I have met many famous people over the years from Cliff Richard to Honor Blackman, but my favourite of all time would have to have been George Thomas, Lord Tonypandy.

We met in the George Thomas Hospice in Cardiff one Christmas. I had to walk with him in the gardens as we were being filmed and I asked him, 'What do I call you?' and he answered, 'Call me George.' We chatted for hours and he invited me to switch the lights on in Cardiff. As a matter of fact we pushed the button together. One of the first things George asked me was, 'Do you still have your mother?' and when I told him, 'Yes,' he looked up and sighed. 'Oh, my mother,' he said, 'Chris, always look after your mother,' and then he started to get quite teary. He adored his mother.

George and I became great friends over the years and spent many times in functions chatting over times past. When he died I was so saddened, but so pleased and proud that I had met and befriended him. He is so sadly missed today by me and Wales.

When Iris Williams came over to Wales to receive her fellowship from the Welsh College of Music and Drama, she and her son, Blake, stayed with me in my flat in Cardiff Bay. It was a special time as it was nearing Christmas and it turned out to be fantastic.

We reminisced over times past, as I'd first met Iris in the early 70s at the Sandman Club on Aberafan beach and had played for her with my buddies, Aquarius. She'd asked me to pull the piano out front beside her, as if I was her musical director. I never forget her first song. It was 'Without a Song' with a rhythm like 'Don't Rain On My Parade'. We really hit it off that week. The great Iris Williams stood next to my piano in my home town...wicked!

David and Sally

One of the most important friends in my life has to be David Emanuel, famous for designing Princess Di's wedding dress. The first time I met him we were singing at the Eisteddfod and I asked him if he would mend the hem of my trousers as it had come down, which he readily agreed to do. What a great man, what a great Welshman. I always thought that he might be too well-to-do for me, perhaps, but how wrong could I be? I can sum him up in a word: *'dude'*. And a fabulous one at that!

David loves to come to my house and enjoys food and chatting. He also enjoys coming to my shows and has even performed in one or two. He has now become the patron of my hospital appeal; he's simply a great guy and deserves a medal the size of a manhole cover. He has the most infectious laugh I have ever heard in my life and what's more he loves to laugh – something I really like. I wish more people would laugh these days.

Sally Burton is always back and fore to Wales and she loves it. I remember asking her once what part of Wales she was from and she said, 'The Chelsea Valleys, dear!' She is one great lady. I first met her when she was starting the Richard Burton 10k run in Cwmafan. I found her so easy to get on with.

I approached Sally one day and asked her to become a patron of the hospital appeal. Without hesitation she said yes and donated Richard's luggage for an auction to kick off the fund raising. What a lovely and generous thing to do.

Not forgetting...

These last few years I have made some new friends, namely Peter Karrie, aka Gentleman Pete, and the wonderful Steve Balsamo, and I'm glad to say that I am to record with them soon on my latest album.

I met Peter through *The Contender*, but the first time I met Steve Balsamo was in an Italian restaurant in Cardiff called Servini's. I met him later at St David's Hall with Bonnie Tyler at a big charity do, and then we became good buddies when I worked with Steve and the Storys on *The Big Buzz* in Swansea. He has an amazing voice and even nicer hair. I asked him to help me out by doing a duet on my new CD, and I was really worried asking him, but he simply said, 'Yes. See you in the studio.' I later found out that I used to work with his father Luigi in the Townsman club in Swansea, Luigi was the head waiter there, and served amazing food.

I met Sue Roderick in the late 80s and we became great friends. Once we went to Porthmadog to do a show, and I played for her and she sang. I noticed that when the show was over and she was talking North Walian to someone, she was responding to them by breathing in, like a sigh but back to front. I have now adopted this gulp and have proudly named it the North Walian Gulp. Thank you, Sue Rod, for that and for always holding a flag for me.

I can't leave out one lady in particular, my Pearl Barley. Sadly she is no longer with us. Pearl was a wonderful lady from Llanelli who was always an angel on my shoulder. I only met her once but I knew that she thought the world of me and always called me her angel.

When my first television programme, *The Chris Needs Experience*, was broadcast it was on the digital channel BBC 2W and many people simply didn't have digital television at the time. Pearl decided to make copies of the programme and sent them out, free of charge to everyone who wanted a copy. Pearl took over the role of mother for me and treated me like her own son.

My mother also had a good friend called Gloria, and she lived somewhere in Neath and has always been in my mind. She was so kind to me when I was young, but we lost touch with each other. I'll always remember her kindness to me, she really did understand me, and I would love to maybe meet up with her again perhaps in the future. Thank you, Gloria. If you read this – please get in touch!

A few years ago I was introduced to a man called Paul Needs. Naturally I asked if he was related to me and apparently he is, a couple of times removed on my father's side. Paul has done a lot for me with his computer skills, with my website, etc, and is now quite settled in the land of the moving curtains with his new lady from Scotland, Beth. Paul also plays guitar and sings and now works answering the phones on my programme. He likes the name Needs, but as for me, you know the rest. I can't stand the name.

Gwenda Owen is one of the sweetest ladies I have ever met. She comes from Carmarthenshire, and is a singer, mainly in Welsh, who I got to know while working on Radio Cymru. I met Gwenda quite often. Sometimes she would come to the studio, or I would meet her on an outside broadcast and we became good chums.

What I like the most about Gwenda is her honesty and her humility. One day outside the BBC in Cardiff she approached me in tears. She had just been told that she had breast cancer, and boy was she upset. My natural instinct was to cwtch her, which I did, and we talked for ages still standing outside the Beeb.

To help her a little I rattled off a list of people who I knew had survived this awful disease and I am delighted to think this calmed her down a lot. She knew what lay ahead of her and I appreciated just what this entailed. I already knew there were different grades of cancer, and I've heard so many people talk of radium treatment and chemotherapy and this gave a glimmer of hope to Gwenda.

She went on to have treatment and became a crusader. She would go on air, both radio and television, to talk about the situation, which must have been such a comfort for so many other women in her position.

I'm glad to say that Gwenda is now doing fine, just as Nurse Needs expected. Some time later I invited Gwenda and her husband Emlyn to my house to celebrate my MBE. During the evening Gwenda presented me with a poem she had written. It was in a posh frame as well and read:

To Chris Needs on the occasion of his receiving the MBE

If the powers to be were inclined to bestow their honours for friendship and charm,
For the wisdom to welcome the world with a smile, and the grace to keep loved ones from harm,
Then Chris Needs would already have medals galore, and titles beyond compare,
And no need to travel to London town to receive all the accolades there.
So Chris, when you're ready, and rightly regaled, and standing in front of the Queen,

She'll tell you, 'This honour's for services past, to
broadcasting, radio and screen.'
If she only knew of the qualities rare, that you share with
whomever you can,
She'd be saying along with your friends, and your fans,
Cometh the hour, cometh the man,

Emlyn and Gwenda.

This means so much to me, thank you Emlyn. Diolch, Gwend!

CHAPTER 13

Needs in a Nutshell

THIS CHAPTER IS ALL about my intimate bits. No, not those, but the little things that are meaningful in my life.

FIRSTS

My first childhood memory

... IS OF ME on a beach somewhere in Wales walking around the rocks in the shallow part of the sea with my mother and father looking for crabs.

Another memory I have is from when I was about 18 months old, perhaps a little older, and I was in the big bed with my mother. She was sound asleep and I wanted to do Number Twos. I couldn't wake her, so I tried to climb over her head to get out of the bed to go to the toilet. The bed was against the wall but I didn't make it and ended up doing it on my mother's head. What a way to wake her up, eh!

My first record

...was 'The Ying Tong Song' by The Goons. It was on a 78 and my father walked to Neath to buy it as the car was broken and he couldn't be bothered to wait for the bus, which came every hour or so.

The first film I remember

...is *The Red Balloon*, about a little boy who sees a balloon which follows him around everywhere and it becomes his friend. Set in France, it's a dumb film in the sense that there's no actual dialogue. The usual thing happens in that other kids get jealous and take the balloon away from him and destroy it. In the end, all the other balloons in France slip away from their owners and go to the boy who is rightly upset and they all gather and take the boy up into the air – then it finishes.

My first date

...was a total disaster. I quickly learned NOT to put all my eggs in one basket and put all my trust in one person. He ran out on me, and left me to carry the can. My mother always said, 'You can live with someone for 50 years and still not know them.' How right she was.

My first TV programme

...was called *Showcase* and it was an HTV production. Back in the 1970s I was doing as many shows as possible when I had a call from a television producer called Terry Delacey. He told me he was interested in putting me on TV to sing two songs. It was a big thing for me. Chris Needs from Cwmafan going on telly. This was about December 1977 and I heard nothing more over the Christmas period but each day I hoped that Terry would call me back. The call came in January and a little while after I went to the HTV studios in Pontcanna, Cardiff, with a white suit in hand and my mother in the audience. The show was a great success. At the time I was resident organist at the Taibach Workingmen's Club in Port Talbot and when I walked in to the club the day after the whole of the club stood up and clapped. My God, was that the start of opening a can of worms. After that there was no stopping me – showbiz here I come!

FAVOURITES

My favourite toy

…was actually not a toy but, as I've already said, the boxes they all came in. They would keep me amused for hours. I would make a den out of the box and slept in them quite often.

I also loved my Pelham puppets. I had a clown and a Dutch boy and a Dutch girl and remember putting on shows like in *The Sound of Music*, only I did it first, ha, ha! I loved my post office, chemistry set and I remember my mother asking me outside a toy shop in Station Road, Port Talbot, what I wanted and I chose something that cost 19/6d. (97.5p) She promptly replied, 'Do you think your father owns the steelworks? Not a thing over ten shillings (50p) this year my boy.'

I also had a small panda bear called Poosey and loved him with all of my heart. I took him everywhere with me and always in bed. One night I was sick all over him and my poor mother had to wash him right down, but it never put me off him, I still loved Poosey just as much.

My favourite television programmes

…as a child were *Torchy The Battery Boy* and, of course, *The Woodentops*. I'm sure to this day that Sam the farm hand was giving more than eggs to Mummy Woodentop. He always managed to sling his hook as Daddy Woodentop returned. *Twizzle* was another favourite, as was *Sara and Hoppity*. I think I still walk like Hoppity.

I watch *Fireball Xl5* now on tape, as well as *Supercar* and *Stingray*. I have the box sets complete of *Mile High* and *Space 1999*, and I adore *The Champions*. *The Saint* was another favourite of mine, the one with Roger Moore of course, as well as *The Avengers*, *Fame* and *Bergerac*, but my favourite of all time has to be the ill-fated soap *Eldorado*. I loved watching *The Wheel Tappers and Shunters Club* even though I'm not a fan of clubs, due to the abuse I got from real men. There were some great acts on that show and I loved Bernard Manning.

These days I love talent shows, like *Joseph* and *Maria*. There's also a programme on satellite about Swiss train journeys which is brilliant. I used to watch *House Doctor*, but I got fed up of so many chavs having their houses done up. I like to watch *The Weakest Link*. I think that Anne Robinson is ace and I get really annoyed when the Welsh have a go at her. I know what she said – but she was winding us up. And she does it so well, so much so that a lot of people here have taken the bait. She really is a pussy cat.

I also love Spanish soaps and *Hollyoaks*. I really dig the people in that show; they are all so good looking. I have a soft spot for the McQueen family. They are so chav but I love them to bits, especially John Paul, a really nice character who's gay and does an amazing job kissing Craig, his mate, who's still seeing his girlfriend. I don't know if they are really gay in real life but they really have convinced me. Nice one, lads!

My favourite films

...could take for ever to list so I'll just jot down a few of my overall favourites.

Sister Act 1 and *2*; anything with Arnold Schwarzenegger or Steven Seagal; the *Die Hard* films, the *Carry On* films and anything made in England at Borehamwood, Elstree or Pinewood Studios. I love the old black and white films with people like Dirk Bogarde. I liked that era and Britain in those days. I'm not so fussed now! Then I love *Escape from East Berlin*, *Berlin Tunnel 21*, *Night Crossing*...

My favourite item of clothing

...has to be my leather trousers, with a massive belt with the word 'ROCK' on the buckle. I wore these to the Eisteddfod in Pencoed. Boy, did heads turn that day.

My favourite musical

Miss Saigon.

My favourite male singer

Billy Ocean. I don't know why, but I've always loved his disco-style music – though I wasn't fussed on his hair back in the 70s as it was too much like mine.

My favourite female singers

Mandy Starr, Bonnie Tyler and Anastacia.

My favourite groups

Abba, Rolling Stones and Earth, Wind and Fire.

My favourite Welsh artiste

Steve Balsamo.

My favourite place in Wales

Tintern.

Favourite seaside resort

Newgale.

Favourite place in UK

London.

Favourite places in Europe

Gibraltar and Jersey.

Favourite country

Anywhere hot, maybe Peru or Mexico.

Favourite language

Spanish.

Favourite chip shop

When I lived in Cardiff I always went to get chips in Clark's in Clifton Street. The shop was run by Mrs Clark and I was treated like a star when I went there.

Favourite meal
Paella.

My least favourite meal
Offal.

My favourite meat
Pork.

Favourite vegetable
Courgette.

My favourite drink
Tea.

My favourite colour
Black.

My favourite animal
Anything as long as it's on a plate. I'm not an animal person.

My favourite joke
I was in chapel one Sunday evening and there were not many people there. So I put a £50 note in the collection and later the minister asked, 'Who put this in the collection box?' So I said, 'It was me.' The minister said that was very generous of me and in return for this gesture I could choose two hymns. So I said, 'I'll have him and him.'

MY AWARD CEREMONY BIRTHDAY BASH

When I was forty-something, I got my age wrong for a long time. I was a year out. I'd think I was 45 when I was 44. Anyway I decided to throw a big party, so I booked a restaurant in Cardiff city centre, ordered the most elaborate buffet, with prawns cooked in garlic and what-have-you, flew in my friends from all over the UK and from abroad and put them all up in hotels.

I had arranged a do to play my top 100 songs, and I put on an award ceremony with categories like Best Actress To Play A Dead Person (Sue Roderick won that, because she had recently been in a body bag in one of her TV dramas.) Best Producer went to Bethan, Ryan Davies' daughter, for producing such a beautiful baby. There was also message recorded from America from Iris Williams saying that she was so sorry that she couldn't be with us and thanking us for her award.

There were flowers and gold envelopes, with Mari Griffith and Nicky Piper reading out the nominations, there were stretch limos outside and a red carpet on the way in. There were photographers with cameras flashing everywhere and the whole thing was filmed by a producer who worked at the BBC.

I felt like Catherine Zeta and, boy, was I on form. I'm the first to admit, I'm a wild child and I don't do normal, neither do I do straight forward. I have a copy of the bash on video tape, my goodness there were hundreds of celebs there. It was incredible.

MY 50TH BIRTHDAY BASH

I've always been known to give a good bash, but as this big birthday grew closer I gave it no thought. I think to be honest I was afraid of it. I'm afraid of getting old and afraid of being ill.

I was reminded by Gabe that I should celebrate and at that time I was in the flat in Atlantic Wharf, Cardiff, but there was no room to swing a cat (no letters from Animal Rights, please).

My butty, Allan Davey, suggested that I book a club, so I did. We booked the Lawn Tennis Club at Cardiff Castle. They did a really nice buffet, and I arranged flamenco dancers that were really terrific, and guests were all given castanets on the way in. There were drag acts, a DJ, and a whole load of celebs, many of whom sang during the evening, such as the amazing Holly Holyoake and Gillian Elisa, to name but a few. Holly and Gill have always supported me with my shows, and I thank them for that. And watch out for Holly, she's really moving upwards towards superstardom, trust me on that! I always want her to be my friend, she's such a nice a girl, and her family are ace towards me.

Peggy, Gabe's mum, held court with the drag acts, advising and swapping make-up and costume tips. She really was in her element and treasures their group photographs.

Again I flew my friends down to Cardiff and put them all up, I think I spent about £3,000 on the whole thing (should have gone for a quiet meal!) During the party, people were asked to 'All stand for Chris Needs' and the DJ played 'God Save The Queen'. I loved it. It was a night to remember, and I'm glad that I do.

POORER TIMES

I remember staying with the family of a friend of mine in Camberley, Surrey. It was quite a posh area, and when I went to have a bath, I asked for some Fairy Liquid as we all used to use washing up liquid to bathe in. The posh lady of the house said to me, 'Oh, you poor thing'. But I preferred it.

If my mother was broke she would jump in her big posh car and borrow her friend's dog, stick him in the back seat and pull up outside the butchers and ask for bones for the dog. She'd get a load of bones from the butcher, take them home and make soup out of them.

THE WORLD ACCORDING TO CHRIS

Politics?
Probably the best cabaret show I've seen in this country.

Global warming?

Where's the warm bit, I want to know? I've had the central heating on this year right through the supposed summer months. To me, global warming is just a name to call something that's not understood. I firmly believe that here in Britain we are punished from above for all of the bad things that are done: wars, crime, jealousy, unruly behaviour, etc. You only get out what you put in. To wake up in the morning and see an array of luxuries like cloud, rain, snow, hail, floods, gale-force winds, tornados and more rain? I rest my case.

What annoys me?

Restrictions – when I was young, there seemed to be hardly any. We were out playing in the streets and enjoying ourselves. No phones, no fears, and I miss those days. Today you can't even have a fag indoors or you are fined. If I was still smoking there would be riots. Then you HAVE to wear a seatbelt or you are fined. You cannot go just over the speed limit, there are vans out to book you. You cannot use a phone in the car while driving. I do wonder where freedom of speech went. People are frightened to say anything today in case they get sued for it.

How little care people show for others today – for example, if you were dying on a bus stop, it's more than likely someone passing would say, 'I'm late for work.'

Prices – take petrol, for instance. If you put the price of petrol up, everything goes up. I'll never forget the country coming to a standstill over a couple of pence on a litre of petrol. It would be nice to have someone on our side for a change.

The weather – why do we have to have so much rain and cold weather here? Why can't we have a HOT summer for a change? I'm envious of people living in southern Europe, they have it all. Virtually everything is cheaper and the sun shines like the clappers.

People who have faked an accident just to get compensation

– something that's shoved down our throats every time you put the television on.

Adverts on TV about clearing debt – they just get me down.

Jealous people – believe you me I meet a fair share. I remember someone writing to me and asking why I have a boat. The answer is because I got a career, worked hard and anyone who does that can buy what they like. The day I ask someone to pay for my luxuries, will be the day of all days.

Drunkenness – another of my pet hates. I'm frightened to walk the streets of Cardiff or Swansea at night as I have been attacked a few times. I would love to ban alcohol completely, it causes so many problems. How can you reason with someone when they are blotto?

Hearing youngsters who say things like, 'I'm not getting a job. My father never did and if you do you have to pay council tax.' Don't worry chaps, I'll keep you.

Political correctness – when I went to Bahrain once I wore a massive gold cross, and the Bahrainis, who are mostly Muslim, kept saying that it was very beautiful. It's strange that here in the UK people get told to remove such adornments as it can be offensive to others. I can't abide the idea that you cannot have Christmas lights up in towns, that they have to be Festive lights, and that some schools can't hold Carol Services now as it will affect non-Christians. How sad is that? Maybe it's time to change my name from Christopher to Festiver, after all, I want to be proper and correct!

I could go on and on and on…

SPEAKING PERSONALLY

My best feature

Well, here's the shortest section in the book – I'm extremely generous, so generous I don't know when to stop. I love to love, and to care. I'm a God-fearing person and I'm honest and faithful.

My worst feature

From the shortest to what could become the longest section. I hate the way I look and I hate my voice as well as...yes, you've guessed it by now, my hair. I don't like my figure, it's like a three-tier wedding cake. I don't like being insecure and I believe that came from the pig of a man who abused me when I was a child.

I despise my freckles. I loathe being a diabetic. I hate having asthma and I wish I didn't have flat feet. I went to visit a chiropodist once and he asked me to walk up and down about six times barefooted. He said he'd never seen anyone before in his career that had flatter feet than me.

My body is like a baby's bum, I don't really have hair under my arms. People even ask me if I shave under my arms. I don't!

I have thin arms and thin legs. I also have a flat bottom, which I believe came from sitting on organ stools for so many years. I have a double chin and I'd like to be taller.

I'm untidy, outspoken. I interrupt. I moan. I'm never satisfied. I love to argue and every morning I have a go at the way this country is. I must be a nightmare to live with. Nothing is ever good enough. I'd hate to work for me.

I can't stop checking things over and over, I'm quite a compulsive person. When I lock a door, I have to swear badly. Later on, when I'm out traipsing around and I think to myself, did I lock the door? I remember the bad words I said. I also use this method while turning off the iron and my straightening tongs. I repeat myself over and over again.

I also snore so bad that Gabe and I have had to sleep in separate flats. Once I was in a hotel in Jersey with a lady co-presenter in the next room to me, and she had to be moved because of the noise of my snoring.

My biggest regret

...is not having a child.

My most cherished possession

...is my mother's yellow vase from the 1940s. I talk to it often.

My biggest nightmare

...is not having a job or not being able to contact an audience.

What makes me smile

...are genuine people like Gabe and Sammy.

What makes me laugh

...are women and their factory jokes.

I admire

...people who work hard.

I am superstitious of

...Magpies. If there's only one I say, 'How's your family, Mr Magpie?'

My biggest hate in life

...is rain.

If I won the lottery

...you'd have a job to find me. Go south, Chris, go south!

If I didn't have to work this week

...I'd be in Spain.

If I came back in a second life

...I'd like to be Sharon Osbourne's dog.

If I was someone else

...I'd most like to be someone continental with straight hair and tall.

WHAT NEXT AFTER THIS BOOK

...maybe a book on the Garden members and maybe a book on the Jenkins's – Wales' first family.

A MOTTO (OR TWO) THAT BEST SUMS ME UP ME:

- *Laugh and the world laughs with you, cry and they laugh twice as loud.*

- *If you can't dazzle them with brilliance, baffle them with bullshit.*

- *As one door closes, another one slams on your other hand.*

- *A rolling stone gathers no basket of eggs in a bush.*

- *(On my tomb stone)...Out of the rain at last.*

- *If it's not broken, don't mend it. Try and find something else in the house to claim on.*

- *If someone asks you for money for food in the street saying, 'Please, I haven't eaten for four days,' I tell them, 'I wish I had your willpower.'*

But the number one for me is: 'The world is his who enjoys it.' This was a saying I found on a paperweight in a shop in Gibraltar. I went in and saw it and fell in love with it. Unknown to me, Gabe sneaked back into the shop and bought it, and kept it until the following Christmas. I was so overwhelmed when I saw it. Thank you, Gabe.

CHAPTER 14

The Future

Trouble wherever I go

MY LIFE CHANGES SO much I can hardly predict what I'm going to be doing in 10 minutes time, let alone start planning plan for the future. In show business it's not easy to plan anything at all. Unlike most other jobs this is one business where you cannot predict a thing. Yes, you can hope, you can pray, but you can be popular one day and not the next. And if your face doesn't fit... well, my advice is to go and work in a bank, because if you think show business is glamorous, then think again, love. You need nerves of steel.

I have always needed to be doing something in music, whether it's DJ-ing, compering or broadcasting, but a little job in the travel business? Mmm, maybe, what a great thought! Whatever the future holds I always live for today. Who knows what tomorrow will bring?

I really believe that I'm not going to make tomorrow, and I have just reason for saying that, based on my family history. I know it's a well-used phrase, but none of us know what's around the corner.

I recall walking home one night from the Marriott Hotel in Cardiff when this fella grabbed me and held me at knife point. He demanded I give him some money. I just bolted. I got away with it but was very lucky. Others are not always as fortunate.

Not long ago I was attacked outside Newcastle Airport. I

was going to visit my friend and have a few days to recover after a hernia operation. No sooner had I got off the plane, collected my bags and was heading away from the airport than I was robbed and kicked. I was not in best of health, and still in pain from the operation. The kicking burst the stitches and, as you can imagine, left me in a lot of discomfort. Why are there such nasty people around?

Then there was the incident in Benidorm. I had only been in Spain for an hour or so when four men came on to ask me for a light. They stole my two gold chains, one of which belonged to my mother, and then they stabbed me in the leg. I flew back home by return flight and went to work that night, stabbed leg and all. What annoyed me about this incident was not the value of what they stole, but the fact that they took my dear mother's chain. That will give me grief for all time. It can never be replaced – it was something I could not put a monetary value on.

So you see, I seem to attract trouble wherever I go. And in this lousy world in which we live you cannot predict from one day to the next. But thank goodness we can dream about the sort of future we'd like. At least it gives us a goal to strive for.

If my present lifestyle came to an end tomorrow I wouldn't be upset, I wouldn't be angry; I wouldn't feel the pain or be troubled by it. In many respects I think quite the opposite.

The next time around

If I ever came back to this world in another time I would want to be taller, slimmer, have straight hair and be living in the Med. I would love to come back the next time as a male model, having photos taken of me in a G-string and people queuing to see me. I could even become a male escort, and pose everywhere. I'd want to have tanned skin, mind.

I'd want people to fancy me and drool over me. I'd want to

live in a beach house and have a foreign accent. I'd want to be somewhere where they eat Parma ham and melon, rather than greasy chips. It might even be nice to be the head of a travel company and swan around resorts checking things out.

There is, however, one job I fantasize over, one which I almost got to do for a television programme before health and safety reared its ugly head. I'd love to be a trolley dolly – you know, one of those the people who work on airplanes selling food and luxury goods. And pointing out the emergency exits to the forward, side and rear. I could be in a different country each day and that would feed my appetite for travel without having to stay in any one place all of the time.

To be honest, I would choose being a trolley dolly above anything else. I'd be dealing with people on holiday. There would be no moaning, just excited people and me flying everywhere and dressed like a nancy boy. My mother and I were very much the same. She always said that we were really travelers and how right she was. So whatever I would be, I would have to be traveling as much as possible, no way stuck in the same wet place, day in day out.

Damn, it's raining again; time to get to work and here I am, the tortured soul of the century, dreaming of what might be.

I seriously think I would like to be abroad once more. I really do feel at home in Spain. I love Wales, but I miss the weather abroad. I would really love to live abroad, have a gay club and become mine host, maybe the re-incarnation of Larry Grayson. Whyever not?

I also miss not having children. I believe I would have made a wonderful father. I feel I have so much to give. Next time around I'll make sure I read the manual properly. But I count my blessings because I have good friends that I can always rely on. I have my Garden – God bless them, my little Sammy who I adore, and of course the support of Gabe and family. I also thank the Lord for the little bit of half-tidy health I still have.

Don't forget, Lord, my vital statistics for the next time around – taller please, taller.

And I'd like to end my days up the Graig (on the mountain side in Cwmafan) in a hacienda, built on the ground my mother left me, near to where she was born. Then I could look down the valley of Cwmafan and say, 'That's where it all started'.

We publish a wide range of books of Welsh interest. For a full list of publications, why not order our new, free Catalogue? Or you may order books directly from our website:

www.ylolfa.com

TALYBONT CEREDIGION CYMRU SY24 5AP
ebost ylolfa@ylolfa.com
gwefan www.ylolfa.com
ffôn 01970 832 304
ffacs 832 782